lemongrass
and sweet basil

lemongrass
and sweet basil

Khamtane Signavong

NEW HOLLAND

Dedication
In memory of our good friend
Chirawat Siripongvirush

First published in 2004 by
New Holland Publishers (UK) Ltd
London • Cape Town • Sydney • Auckland

Garfield House
86–88 Edgware Road
London W2 2EA
www.newhollandpublishers.com

80 McKenzie Street
Cape Town 8001
South Africa

Level 1, Unit 4
14 Aquatic Drive
Frenchs Forest, NSW 2086
Australia

218 Lake Road
Northcote
Auckland
New Zealand

2 4 6 8 10 9 7 5 3 1

Text and recipe copyright © 2004 Khamtane Signavong and Alison Plummer
Copyright © 2004 photographs Ken Martin and Alison Plummer
Copyright © 2004 New Holland Publishers (UK) Ltd

ISBN 1 84330 741 3

Senior Editor: Clare Hubbard
Editor: Anna Bennett
Designer: Sara Kidd
Photography: Ken Martin
Production: Ben Byram-Wigfield
Editorial Direction: Rosemary Wilkinson

Reproduction by Pica Digital PTE Ltd, Singapore
Printed and bound by Times Offset (M) Sdn. Bhd., Malaysia

contents

Introduction **6**

Ingredients **10**

Methods & Techniques **14**

Central Thailand **18**

Isan – the Northeast **58**

Northern Thailand **82**

The South **102**

Thai "Tapas" **122**

Stocks, Sauces & Relishes **138**

Index **142**

About Khamtane Signavong **143**

Acknowledgements **144**

Introduction

Being Thai is a way of life, from our Thai Buddhist religion to the customs and traditions passed down through generations. Food plays a very large role in our day-to-day living – you could say we have a passion for eating – but there is more involved than merely satisfying our taste buds. The importance of the process of preparation, care in presentation, the essential balance of flavours, as well as the spiritual significance of food, are all part of what might be called the whole "Thainess" of the experience whether the meal features the elaborate detail of Royal Thai Cuisine (so-called because in the past this type of cooking was prepared in the Palace's Inner Court and served only to royals and artistocrats) or is a simple snack from a street stall.

Every day at dawn in Thailand, monks in saffron-coloured robes file out from their monasteries and *wats* (temples) carrying their alms bowls, which are filled by people who wait to give them food, especially precious rice (*khao*), which is at the heart of Thai life. We don't give alms every day but do so as often as possible, wherever we are in the world. The idea is, loosely, that giving the best of what you have to the monks and to your elders and guests will earn you spiritual good marks – and food is a valuable part of the currency.

After the initial greeting (men say *sawadee khap*, women say *sawadee kha*), the next thing that Thais will say, before any further words are exchanged, is "Have you eaten yet?" The time of day doesn't make any difference to the Thai desire to offer you food and I think that Western people may find this strange. Thais have no set mealtimes, often eating about five times a day, enjoying single dishes and snacks as well as main meals. We love to eat in groups, sharing dishes which combine to make a properly balanced meal and incorporate the four vital flavour characteristics of Thai food – spicy, salty, sweet and sour. Understanding this balance is the first step towards creating Thai dishes yourself.

Evening at Wat Phra That Doi Suthep near Chiang Mai.

Here are the basic ingredients we use to achieve the famous four Ss.

Spicy – chillies, peppers, fresh and dried spices, shallots, garlic.

Salty – fish sauce, soy sauce, dried shrimps, shrimp paste, salt.

Sweet – coconut milk, palm sugar, fruit.

Sour – lime juice, tamarind, vinegar, vegetables.

What to cook is the next decision and Thai meals differ from those in Western countries in that they typically include several dishes to share:

Rice
Curry
Soup
Salad
Stir-fry
Dipping sauce with fresh or steamed vegetables
Grilled or barbecued meat, poultry or fish
Chilli with fish sauce
Iced water

The recipes in this book are intended to serve four people as part of a Thai meal – in a restaurant four people would order four different dishes or more, depending on how hungry they are and how much they can afford. The dishes are always placed in the centre of the table, to share, so everyone has a reasonable amount of everything. More dishes are ordered as necessary.

The number of dishes ordered works out at roughly one per person, and rice is always central to the meal. At the restaurant we have a Western-style menu with appetizers, soups, main courses and

desserts listed individually and at home you can serve courses separately as I realize that soup served with a main course is not usual. Noodles, such as the famous *pad thai* noodles, may be served on their own and Thai snacks (*khap klaem*) served with drinks are also separate from a main meal.

My mother used to tell me that when you cook you must ensure you buy the best, freshest ingredients and the right quantity of food to go round. She also taught me that chilli, palm sugar, fish sauce and shrimp paste are all seasonal, and that their taste and heat also depend on the brands you buy, which will vary in the amount of salt and chilli they include. One thing people often ask is whether all Thai dishes have to be hot and spicy by definition. The answer is that not all are, but because we love chilli and spices so much I recommend that you use them to taste. Leaving them out altogether would upset the fine balance of the recipe.

I grew up with a mother and grandmother who went to the markets every morning, buying everything fresh for the day's meals in the traditional Thai way, and at night we would all go to the markets for mangoes, sticky rice, desserts and fruit. Now that I

Chilli dipping sauces are served with steamed or fresh vegetables.

am running a restaurant it is my turn to go round the markets in order to select the best local produce.

For daily shopping go with an open mind as Thais have always done, searching the markets for fresh produce such as meat, seafood and fresh vegetables and looking out for seasonal specials. Of course you must plan ahead for special occasions and Thais like to be prepared, always having their own herb gardens growing chilli, lemongrass, a lime tree, kaffir limes, galangal, mint, basil, shallots, coriander and everything they possibly can for absolute freshness.

Thais are lucky because Thailand is incredibly rich in food resources, with a climate so suitable for growing rice that a harvest is possible twice a year. Because of the abundance of water in the Central and Northern regions, many fruits and vegetables are grown, including cool-climate varieties such as asparagus, strawberries and mangetout. River prawns and river fish are plentiful, as well as seafood from Thailand's long coastlines, and prawn and fish farms export their produce worldwide. The ingredients used in this book are available around the world – a few may take some tracking down through specialist suppliers but you will find them.

You will notice in the regional sections that many influences have come to bear on Thai cooking, from the cuisine and techniques of the Royal Palace to those from neighbouring Laos, Cambodia, Myanmar and Malaysia. The exchanges of culture and trade between Thailand and these countries bordering it have helped Thailand to raise its standard of living. Traders introduced spices and Chinese immigrants arriving in the eighteenth and nineteenth centuries brought noodles and beansprouts, together with techniques such as stir-frying, steaming and roasting, their cooking skills laying the foundations of Central regional cooking. If Thai food has been slow to make

Selecting fresh produce at the Chiang Mai morning markets.

its name around the world I think it may be because the country has never been colonized as the French did Vietnam, the Dutch Indonesia or the British India.

Thai food is now known and appreciated around the world and I am happy to share some ideas for recipes with you from our kitchens at the Arun Thai in Sydney. As is the case in most cultures, Thais learn their cooking skills from their elders and so the techniques come easily.

After a time you will develop your own Thai taste, knowing how to add more or less of the four Ss – spicy, salty, sweet and sour – to create the right flavour for the right dish.

www.arunthai.com.au

Ingredients

Aubergines *(Makeua)*
There are many varieties of aubergine, including baby aubergines, which have a bitter taste, and crispy aubergines the size of golf balls, both used in green curries and with *nam prik* dipping sauce. Long aubergines and purple aubergines are used in stir-fries and salads and, if small or crispy aubergines are unavailable, they can also be used in green chicken curries. Pea aubergines (*makeua puong*) or cherry aubergines are the size of large peas and come in bunches. Slightly bitter and crunchy, they give curry an extra texture. Thai aubergines (*makeua piao*) are the size of golf balls, crunchy in texture but a little less bitter than pea aubergines.

Bamboo shoots *(Nor mai)*
Fresh, young bamboo shoots should be peeled and sliced prior to cooking. If you use tinned bamboo shoots you should drain them and boil them for about 5 minutes in fresh water otherwise they can have a metallic taste.

Preserved or pickled bamboo shoots *(Nor mai dong)*
Mostly used in red and Southern yellow curries (*gaeng leung*), they come in jars, preserved in vinegar, and should be washed thoroughly in cold water before use.

Banana *(Gluay)*
Many varieties of banana are grown all over Thailand. We use sugar bananas for desserts and deep-fry them for banana chips.

Banana blossom or banana flower *(Hua pee)*
This is the large bud at the end of the banana plant. Only the inside is used. Banana blossoms are available, either fresh or preserved, at specialist Asian grocery shops. Only a stainless steel knife should be used to cut fresh banana blossoms as any other metal causes discolouration. Do not prepare more than half an hour in advance. Soak preserved banana blossoms in cold water and rinse before use.

Banana leaf *(Bai dthong)*
Thais use banana leaves to wrap food for steaming and grilling, and for wrapping up desserts such as sticky rice with banana. Before the introduction of the plastic bag, banana leaves were used for carrying fresh food.

Basil
Thai sweet basil differs from other types of basil and is worth seeking out – or growing – to add an authentic Thai flavour to many dishes. If Thai, holy or lemon basil are unavailable, substitute the more widely available Mediterranean variety.

Holy basil *(Bai kaprow – L. Ocinum sanctum)*
Pungent, spicy, aromatic and fragrant with reddish-purple hairy stems. Only the leaves are used in dishes such as jungle curries and beef, chicken or lamb stir-fries.

Lemon basil *(Bai manglak - L.Ocinum basilicum 'Citriodorum')*
This is a lighter green than Thai sweet basil and is not used as much as the other two varieties except in Northern regional cuisine and Isan recipes.

Thai sweet basil *(Bai horapa L. Ocinum basilicum 'Thai')*
Thai sweet basil, available from Asian markets or specialist shops, has leaves that are deep green and smaller than European sweet basil (*L. Ocinum basilicum*). You can distinguish Thai sweet basil by its purplish stems and purple-tinged flower buds. It is mixed in at the very end of the cooking stage, to bring out its sweet aniseed flavour. Thai sweet basil can be grown anywhere that has direct, warm sunlight – a summer garden, sunny balcony, kitchen window-sill or greenhouse.

Beancurd *(see Tofu page 13)*

Beans *(Thao fa yao)*
The green beans in Thai cooking are usually the variety known as snake beans or sometimes yard-long beans. They are used in stir-fries, dipping sauces and salads. French beans may be used instead.

Beansprouts *(Tua noork)*
Sprouted from green mung beans, fresh beansprouts are added to noodle dishes, salads, soups and stir-fries.

Betel leaf *(Bai cha puu)*
Known as betel leaf, although not from the actual betel tree, these leaves grow on a low bush and are used for wrapping ingredients. They can also be cut up and added to curries. Also known as wild pepper. Chinese broccoli (see opposite) can be substituted.

Bitter melon *(Mara)*
A bitter-tasting, gourd-like fruit with bumpy, blistered skin. It is used when a true bitter taste is called for in recipes for soups and stir-fries. Bitter melon can also be eaten raw with dipping sauces.

Chillies *(Prik)*
Used for their colour as well as their fragrance and spicy, dynamic heat, chillies, originally introduced to Thailand by

Portuguese traders, feature prominently in Thai recipes. You will find a heat rating for each recipe with the serving information. Many different varieties are grown all over the world, varying in size, colour and heat; Thai chillies are especially aromatic and fragrant. The two we use most are the bird's eye chillies for heat and sky-pointing chillies for colour. In Thailand, bird's eye chillies are some of the hottest available. It is important to carry out a "test run" for all Thai recipes, especially if you are entertaining, in order to gauge the chilli temperature you might achieve – which will still be by trial and error depending on where the chillies are grown. Generally speaking, the smaller the chilli the greater its heat, but this is not always the case! Deseeding chillies reduces their heat a little: wear rubber gloves to do this. Never touch your eyes after handling chillies and wash your hands thoroughly after doing so.

Banana chilli *(Prik yuak)*
Mild and yellowish green in colour, the banana chilli measures up to 14 cm (5½ in) in length.

Bird's eye chilli *(Prik khi nu)*
This is a tiny chilli, measuring up to 2 cm (¾ in) in length. The Thai name means "mouse dropping", which accurately describes its size. These are the hottest of all chillies.

Sky-pointing chilli *(Prik chi fa)*
These chillies are red, green or yellow and measure up to 8 cm (3¼ in) in length. They are often deseeded prior to use.

Yellow chilli *(Prik leung)*
A mild yellow chilli used mainly to add colour to sauces.

Chilli sauce *(Prik or Sriracha sauce)*
This famous chilli sauce comes from the Sriracha area on the coastline south of Bangkok. Made with vinegar, garlic, chilli and salt, it is added to dishes such as Thai omelettes, oysters and sun-dried beef. For the recipe see page 139.

Dried chilli *(Prik haeng)*
These are whole, sun-dried chillies. Use the large ones for colour, the small ones for heat.

Roasted red chilli paste *(Nam prik pow)*
One of the most important ingredients in recipes from the Central region, this is a combination of shrimp paste, dried hot red chillies, garlic, shallots, tamarind juice and palm sugar with seasoning, used in the famous *Tom Yum Goong* soup (see pages 24–25), Banana Flower Salad (see pages 28–29) and some stir-fries. For the recipe see page 14.

Chinese broccoli *(Kana)*
Also known as Chinese kale, Chinese broccoli has oval leaves on a long, thin stalk. It is used in stir-fries and as a substitute for betel leaves.

Chinese cabbage *(Pak kad kao)*
Chinese cabbage has thin, crinkly leaves and a thick, white stalk. It is used in soups and stir-fries and can be steamed to serve with a dipping sauce. It is also used to wrap fish prior to steaming, to prevent the fish from sticking to the plate in the steamer.

Chinese chives *(Kui chi)*
These have flat leaves and a garlic flavour. Use in *pad thai* noodles and for garnishing.

Cloud ear fungus *(Hed hunuu)*
Also known as wood or black fungus, this grows throughout Asia and is available fresh or dried. It is used in soups, jungle curries and salad. Look out for it dried in Asian grocery shops – it should be soaked in warm water for 30 minutes before using. Field mushrooms may be substituted.

Coconut milk *(Kathi)*
A must in many delicious Thai curries, especially those from the Central region, and also for making desserts. Coconut milk and concentrated coconut cream (*hua kathi*) are made from the ripe flesh of the coconut, which is mixed with warm water and squeezed to form coconut cream. After more water is added, the second press produces coconut milk. (See page 16.)

Coriander *(Pak chee)*
A fragrant member of the parsley family. Thais use the whole coriander plant – leaves, stems, seeds, roots and all. The leaves and stalks are for flavouring, while the roots are

Squid and anchovies drying in the sun at Rayong.

used to flavour marinades and stocks. The seeds are used in curries and in marinades for some meat dishes.

Dried shrimps *(Goong haeng)*
Tiny prawns from the sea off the coasts of Southern Thailand are sun-dried and used to add a salty, fishy flavour to dishes including *pad thai* noodles, salads and soups. They are also used in stocks and to make Roasted Red Chilli Paste (see pages 11 and 14).

Fish sauce *(Nam pla)*
An essential ingredient in Thai cooking, fish sauce is made from small fish, such as anchovies or prawns, fermented in brine. Fish sauce adds a distinctive salty taste to most Thai dishes but some brands have extra salt added which can create an imbalance in the flavours. Look out for those brands that are lower in salt.

Galangal *(Kha)*
An important ingredient in Isan cooking, young, pink-skinned, ribbed galangal rhizomes have white flesh and a distinctly exotic, fragrant, aromatic and peppery taste, great for soups. As galangal ages, the skin darkens and the flavour becomes stronger, making it good for curry pastes.

Garlic *(Kratiam)*
Thai garlic is smaller, more pungent and fragrant than the larger garlic found in other countries, but is not readily available outside Asia so use the freshest garlic you can find locally for cooking Thai food.

Pickled garlic *(Kratiam dong)*
Garlic pickled in vinegar, salt and sugar is used by Thais as a sauce and condiment.

Ginger *(Khing)*
Older ginger roots are used for steamed dishes and stir-fries and younger ginger roots for pickling. The white flowers are eaten with dipping sauce. See also Lesser Ginger, right.

Kaffir lime *(Bai magrood)*
Both the skin of this knobbly lime (the zest of an ordinary lime can be substituted) and its distinctive figure-of-eight leaves are used. The leaves are thinly sliced or torn to add their strong citrus flavour to soups, stir-fries and curries. Dried kaffir lime leaves may be used – double the quantity of fresh required and soak for 15–20 minutes in warm water before using. See also Lime, right.

Lemongrass *(Takrai)*
A stalky grass with a wonderful lemon flavour and fragrance, the outer part is peeled off and only the firm white part inside used. This is crushed for soups, sliced for salads and pounded for curries. Pounding and crushing releases the fragrant oils from these seemingly dry stalks.

Lesser ginger *(Krachai)*
Krachai is used to add a gingery and spicy flavour to curried dishes and, like galangal and kaffir lime (see left), is a good foil for strong-flavoured meats and seafood. Fresh *krachai* has finger-like tubers, brown on the outside and pale yellow inside. Preserved *krachai* is available from Asian grocery shops – it should be rinsed well in cold water before using.

Lime *(Manao)*
One of the main ingredients in Thai cooking, giving the sharp, citrus, "sour" Thai taste in soups, salads and dipping sauces. See also Kaffir lime, left.

Mango *(Mamuang)*
Many varieties of mango are found in Thailand, each varying in size and taste. Hard, unripe green mangoes are peeled and sliced to give a deliciously sour tang to salads and dipping sauces, while ripe mangoes are eaten as a fruit or as a dessert with sticky rice.

Mint *(Bai salanae)*
Thai mint has a small, round leaf and a pungent flavour. Garden mint can be substituted.

Mushrooms *(Hed)*
Mushrooms used in Thai cooking include the small-capped, long-stalked, sweet straw mushroom used in *Tom Yum Goong* soup (see pages 24–25) and stir-fries. Button mushrooms can be substituted for straw mushrooms.

Noodles
Thais eat plenty of noodles, cooked in a variety of ways:

Cellophane or glass noodles *(Wun sen)*
These are made from mung bean flour and are used in soups, salads and spring rolls.

Dried rice noodles *(Guay teow)*
These noodles come in three sizes: large noodles (*sen yai*); medium or rice stick (*sen lek*), like Italian tagliatelle, often used in *pad thai* noodles and noodle soup; and tiny, fine noodles (*sen mee*), like Italian vermicelli, used in noodle soup.

Egg noodles *(Ba mee)*
Made with plain flour, egg and water, they come in medium flat (*sen ban*) or small and fine (*sen ba mee* or *sen bpan*).

Fresh rice noodles *(Kanom jin)*
These are typically served with a selection of sauces and vegetables.

Oil *(Nam mun)*
Animal fat is traditionally used for cooking in Thailand but more health-conscious Thais are now switching to vegetable oils.

Oyster sauce *(Nam mun hoi)*
Made from oyster extract, this sauce has a rich, salty, sweet flavour and a smooth texture. It is mostly used in stir-fries or marinades.

Palm sugar *(Nam tan peep)*
Made from the sap of the coconut or sugar palm and varying from dark brown to almost white. Palm sugar is used to balance dishes and add a sharp sweetness.

Pandanus leaf *(Bai toey)*
Pandanus grows profusely in Thailand and its leaves are widely used in Royal Thai Cuisine to wrap chicken. The fragrant, almost perfumed vanilla flavour goes very well with coconut for desserts. The leaves are inedible and should be discarded before serving.

Papaya *(Ma la kor)*
There are several varieties of papaya in Thailand, with either long or round fruit. The crispy, crunchy green variety which never ripens is shredded for salads in the North and Isan, while in the South it is used in *Gaeng Leung*. Ripe papaya is eaten on its own, and is also dried for use in snacks.

Peppercorns *(Prik thai oan)*
Unripe green peppercorns are used in jungle curries and stir-fries to help to balance the flavours. Ground white pepper is widely used while black pepper is only used in some regional dishes.

Pomelo *(Som o)*
A member of the grapefruit family, the pomelo is a great favourite in salads and is also eaten on its own.

Rice *(Khao)*
Thailand is the home of fragrant, long-grain jasmine rice (*khao horm mali*), which is highly regarded as the staple for most Thai meals throughout Thailand. Sticky or glutinous rice (*khao niaw*) is eaten instead of jasmine rice in the North and Isan regions. Elsewhere it is used in desserts such as the famous sticky rice with mango. Ground, roasted rice is rice which has been dry-fried in a wok with galangal until golden-brown, then ground to a fine powder and used in many Isan and Northern regional dishes.

Shallots *(Hom deng)*
Thai shallots are reddish-purple in colour and are smaller than brown shallots, which can also be used in Thai recipes. Shallots bring out the flavours in curries, curry

pastes including Roasted Red Chilli Paste (see page 14) and dipping sauces. They are also sliced and used in salads.

Shrimp paste *(Gapi)*
Pungent and salty, this is a must-have ingredient in curry paste for its aromatic and preserving qualities. It is made from shrimps mixed with salt, which are dried in the sun, then blended to a paste. Used in curries, dipping sauces and in stir-fries, you can find it in Asian grocery stores.

Soy sauce *(Nam siew)*
Made from fermented soya beans, light soy sauce is salty and aromatic and is used in stir-fries and for soup and marinades; dark soy sauce is sweet and less salty and used in noodle dishes and some Chinese-influenced dishes.

Spring onions *(Ton hom)*
Long, green-stemmed spring onions (or scallions) are mild in flavour and used in stir-fries, salads and soups.

Tamarind *(Mak kam)*
Growing in bunches of pods on the tamarind tree, the fruit is crushed and can be bought pressed in block form or as concentrated tamarind paste. Both can be mixed with water to make tamarind juice, see pages 16–17.

Tofu (Beancurd) *(Taohu)*
Made from the liquid of crushed soya beans, tofu, also known as beancurd, is high in protein and available in a choice of firm or soft. Soft (or silken) beancurd is used in soups or for steaming and roasting. The firm type is good for stir-frying and deep-frying as it keeps its shape while it cooks. Individual recipes specify which kind to use.

Turmeric *(Khamin)*
A root similar to ginger, turmeric is used for its yellow colour as well as its flavour, especially in Southern Thai regional dishes. You can use fresh turmeric root or the more widely available ground turmeric.

Twisted or stink beans *(Sator)*
These large, flat bitter beans are very popular in Southern Thailand. They are served boiled for dipping or used in stir-fries with prawns and shrimp paste.

Wing beans *(Tua phuu)*
Grown in Southeast Asia, these distinctive green beans have a smooth skin with four prominent ridges – when sliced through, each piece is star-shaped. Wing beans are generally used in salads and blanched whole in boiling water to eat with dipping sauces. These beans must be fresh – ask about them in specialist shops.

methods & techniques

Chilli curry pastes

Red and green curry pastes are used as a basis for many Thai dishes, while other pastes are individually blended to create specific dishes such as a Mussaman Beef Curry (see pages 114–115). This pre-blending of herbs and spices is the significant flavour factor in much of Thai cooking.

Made from fresh and dried herbs and spices, each recipe is different depending on the cook and the house style as each household has its own recipes that are passed on from generation to generation. Thais can tell how good you are at making chilli paste by the sound of the pestle and mortar as you pound. Historically wives were selected on their ability to make good chilli paste, but now society has changed and like families all over the world many Thai households buy their paste from supermarkets.

You can do that too, but passionate cooks will not be content without some recipes. You can either make your paste fresh each time or make a quantity and store it for later use if you intend to cook Thai often. It keeps – stored in an airtight, sterilized jar – for up to 3 months in the fridge. To sterilize the jar, wash it thoroughly in warm, soapy water, rinse and dry in a moderate oven for 5 minutes.

You can use an electric coffee grinder kept specifically for spices, a food processor or blender, but the traditional pounding method is best for the real Thai taste. Fresh ingredients make all the difference when you pound as the idea is to release the moist juices in order to form the paste.

When you cook with coconut milk and curry paste you aromatize them by heating until the oil separates and floats to the top before adding other ingredients. Dry seeds such as cumin and coriander are toasted by heating a wok and dry-frying the seeds until they change colour.

The recipes make about 2–4 tablespoons of paste.

Roasted red chilli paste
nam prik pao

4 tablespoons vegetable oil
15 cloves garlic, peeled and chopped
5 shallots, peeled and chopped
5 dried red chillies, deseeded and soaked in warm water
1 teaspoon shrimp paste
1 tablespoon palm sugar
1 tablespoon tamarind juice (see pages 16–17)
1½ teaspoons salt

Heat the oil in a wok over a medium heat, add the garlic and shallots and fry until golden brown. Remove from the heat and set aside.

Add the chillies and fry until brown. In a mortar pound the chillies, garlic, shallots and shrimp paste until fine and return to the wok along with the palm sugar, tamarind juice and salt. Stir-fry over a low heat until the mixture has aromatized and thickened. This paste can be kept in a jar for up to 3 months; top up with vegetable oil to prevent drying.

Gaeng hanglay paste
nam prik gaeng hanglay

1 tablespoon shrimp paste
5 shallots, unpeeled
4 garlic cloves, unpeeled
2 lemongrass stalks, very thinly sliced
1 tablespoon coriander seeds
1 tablespoon cumin seeds
5 large dried chillies, deseeded and soaked in warm water
1 teaspoon ground turmeric
½ teaspoon salt

Preheat the oven or grill to 160°C/325°F/Gas Mark 3. Wrap the shrimp paste in foil, place on a baking tray with the shallots, garlic and lemongrass and bake for 10 minutes. Set aside to cool, then peel off the skins.

In a wok, dry-fry the coriander and cumin seeds over a medium heat until dark brown and fragrant, about 5 minutes. Put the baked ingredients, dry-fried seeds, chillies, turmeric and salt into a mortar and pound to a fine paste.

Chiang mai noodle paste
nam prik gaeng khao soi
5 dried bird's eye chillies, deseeded and soaked in warm water
1 lemongrass stalk
3 shallots, peeled and sliced
2 slices of galangal
2 kaffir lime leaves
½ teaspoon ground turmeric
1 teaspoon grated kaffir (or ordinary) lime zest
5 garlic cloves, peeled and chopped
1 teaspoon coriander seeds

Combine all the ingredients in a mortar and pound to a paste with a pestle. Use a blender if you prefer.

Green curry paste
nam prik gaeng khao wan
1 teaspoon coriander seeds
½ teaspoon cumin seeds
10 green bird's eye chillies or green chillies, chopped
1 stalk lemongrass, finely sliced
2 shallots, peeled and chopped
1 teaspoon sliced galangal
1 teaspoon chopped coriander root
1 tablespoon ground black pepper
2 tablespoons sliced kaffir lime leaves
½ teaspoon grated kaffir lime zest
1 teaspoon shrimp paste
1 teaspoon salt

Toast the dry seeds in a wok and then grind them until fine in a pestle and mortar. Now put the remaining ingredients into the mortar and pound with a pestle until you achieve a paste.

Red curry paste
nam prik gaeng phet
1 teaspoon shrimp paste
1 tablespoon coriander seeds
½ teaspoon cumin seeds
15 big dried chillies, deseeded and soaked in warm water
1 stalk lemongrass, finely sliced
2 teapsoons chopped shallots
1 clove garlic, minced
1 teaspoon grated galangal
1 tablespoon freshly ground black pepper
2 Kaffir lime leaves, sliced
½ teaspoon Kaffir lime zest, finely chopped
1 teaspoon salt

Wrap the shrimp paste in foil and grill for 5 minutes. Toast and grind the dry seeds. Blend all the ingredients together to a paste using either a mortar and pestle or a food processor.

Panang curry paste
nam prik panang
1 tablespoon shrimp paste
1 tablespoon coriander seeds
½ tablespoon cumin seeds
15 big dried red chillies, deseeded and soaked in warm water
2 tablespoons shallots, chopped
3 tablespoons chopped garlic
1 stalk lemongrass, finely sliced
1 teaspoon galangal, sliced
1 tablespoon chopped coriander root
3 tablespoons freshly toasted mung beans, crushed

Wrap the shrimp paste in foil and grill for 5 minutes. Toast the seeds, then blend everything together in a mortar using a pestle to form a fine paste.

Mussaman curry paste

nam prik gaeng mussaman

1 teaspoon coriander seeds
2 cardamom pods
1 teaspoon black peppercorns
1 teaspoon cumin seeds
1 nutmeg
2 cloves
6 big dried red chillies, deseeded and soaked in
 water
4 cloves garlic, peeled and finely chopped
3 shallots, peeled and finely chopped
6 slices of galangal, finely chopped
1 stalk lemongrass, finely chopped
1 teaspoon shrimp paste
2 teaspoons vegetable oil
1 teaspoon salt

Heat the wok over a low heat and add the coriander seeds, cardamom, black pepper, cumin, nutmeg and cloves and dry stir-fry until fragrant, about 4–5 minutes. Remove and set aside to cool. Using the same wok, stir-fry all the remaining ingredients (except the shrimp paste, oil and salt) until fragrant, then remove and set aside to cool.

Put all the spices in a mortar and pound to a fine paste with the pestle. Add all the remaining ingredients and continue to pound to a fine paste. This paste can be stored in a jar in the refrigerator for up to 3 months.

Coconut milk

Coconut milk and coconut cream are available in tins or packs. Coconut milk is the squeezed white flesh of the coconut mixed with hot water. The first pressing produces coconut cream and then the second produces thinner milk. You can buy them individually but you can also separate the cream from a can of coconut milk as, when you open it, you will find the dense cream floating on the top of the milk.
If you want to make it at home 225 g (8 oz) shredded (or desiccated) coconut mixed with 600 ml (1 pt) water produces 450 ml (¾ pt) of coconut milk.

Rice

The cooking time and amount of water required depend on the age of the rice used. Very white rice is generally new and more moist so needs less water. Older rice is more yellow in colour and is harder, so it needs more water.

Jasmine rice – my grandmother rinsed the long-grain jasmine rice three times in fresh water before putting it into a pan and covering it with water. The traditional Thai way of measuring is to place your hand flat over the rice and to add enough water to cover both. Cook from cold, bringing the water to the boil for 7 minutes then simmering until all the water is absorbed, about 15–20 minutes in total.

Sticky or glutinous rice is soaked overnight before cooking, usually by steaming for about 20 minutes. Quantities are always hard to gauge, but as a rule 400 g (13½ oz) jasmine rice in 1 litre (1¾ pt) of cold water serves four, depending on your appetite. In Thailand rice is central to the meal and so we always have plenty on hand. Electric rice cookers are used widely in Thailand.

Shredded pork skin

Buy 200 g (7 oz) pork skin from the butcher. Place the pork skin in a saucepan, add 1½ litres (2¾ pt) water and a pinch of salt and boil for 20 minutes, until tender. Drain and cool, then use a very sharp knife to cut the pork skin into fine strips.

Pork crackers

Buy 200–300 g (7–10 oz) pork skin from the butcher and cut it into long strips, about 2.5 cm (1 in) wide and 5–7.5 cm (2–3 in) long. Heat a wok and fry the pork skin strips for about 20 minutes over a medium heat then remove and allow to dry. Add 500 ml (18 fl oz) oil to the wok and heat. Fry the pork strips until golden-brown and crispy. Remove the pork crackers and drain. Store in a sealed bag or airtight container until required (will keep for 1 week).

Tamarind juice

To make tamarind juice (or tamarind water) soak ⅓ tamarind pulp to ⅔ water, then strain. Tamarind concentrate is also available and is diluted with water, but the tangy flavour of the freshly soaked pulp is more intense.

Stir-frying in a wok

A speciality of Chinese cuisine, brought by immigrants and adopted by the then Siamese, this is the quickest way to cook food – first heating the wok over the gas flame, then adding oil and heating until a haze appears. The hot oil sears the food to preserve freshness. Slicing the food into small pieces helps it to cook quickly and evenly, and of course you add the ingredients which need the longest cooking time first. Stir-fried dishes should be served immediately they are cooked, which usually takes less than 5 minutes.

• Don't add water (or anything damp) to smoking oil as it will create a high flame.

• Don't add garlic or chilli first to the hot oil. Garlic will burn and chilli will give off an overpowering aroma which can make you cough. Either add these two to the oil with the other ingredients or first cook them over a low flame before turning up the heat and adding the other ingredients.

Deep-frying

Thais love deep-fried food cooked until the outside is crispy and the inside still moist and tender. But we are becoming more health-conscious, aware of cholesterol concerns and so on, so there is less deep-frying now. Food should be dry before deep-frying and the oil heated to 150°–185°C (300–360°F) – if less it will be soggy. Over 190°C (370°F) it will burn outside but be raw inside.

Crisp-frying

Ingredients including basil, chillies, garlic, shallots, dried shrimps and fish are crispy-fried for some recipes for texture, flavour and colour. Cook quickly in the wok to crisp them without burning.

Dry pan-frying

Ingredients such as chilli, raw rice, galangal and spices for curries are dry-fried in a wok to achieve a smoky, toasty taste. Heat the wok and add the spices, frying to aromatize, stirring to avoid burning.

Grilling

When Thais say grilling they traditionally mean char-grilling over a low flame to achieve a smoky flavour or over a high heat like a barbecue. At home you can use the grill, oven or barbecue, depending on the requirements of the recipe.

Steaming

I love this healthy method of cooking vegetables, and seafood and sticky rice is always steamed. The water should be boiling before you begin to steam and ingredients such as fish are steamed on a bed of cabbage on a plate. If you have extra thick plates the fish may take longer to cook than the time specified.

Pounding

We still use a traditional stone mortar and pestle for pounding both fresh and dried spices and herbs. Clay mortars are less often used as they break easily and have been replaced by metal ones used with a wooden pestle.

Most ingredients should be chopped before pounding and adding a pinch of salt will stop the juice from wetter ingredients spraying you in the eye. The idea is to pound everything to mash it together – many recipes call for pounding to a paste so you should continue until you have achieved that.

Chopping and slicing

In Thai recipes, food is sliced for salads and stir-fries and chopped into small pieces for curries and other dishes. The bite-sized pieces are quick to cook and easy to eat – Thais use a fork and spoon to eat with rather than a knife, so basically nothing is served that needs further slicing, the preparation has all been done in the kitchen. The intricate and delicate carving of fruit and vegetables in Royal Thai Cuisine is a great skill, an art form which is the result of much practice and the subject of great competition amongst cooks who specialize in it, even today. The carved fruit and vegetables are part of the meal not just for decoration, so eat and enjoy them.

Central Thailand

Fragrant spices & coconut milk

The cuisine of the Central region is probably the best-known internationally, with an emphasis on sweeter, more subtle flavours rather than the spicier, hotter tastes of dishes from the South or from Isan.

Coconut milk and the famous red and green curry pastes are essentials for dishes such as Green Chicken Curry (see pages 32–33). Prawns are widely used and duck is a favourite, a result of the Chinese influence here. Some of the well-known Thai soups come from the Central region, including King Prawn Soup with Chilli and Lime (see pages 24–25), Chicken and Coconut Soup (see pages 26–27), as well as noodle dishes such as Stir-fried Rice Noodles with King Prawns (see pages 52–53).

Thai people eat four or five times a day and, because food is relatively cheap, fresh and plentiful, they tend to eat out. Most eat locally but Thais are happy to travel if they know the food will be good, and they love to eat somewhere famous. All types of produce are readily available in the centre of the country as the network of rivers and canals creates a fertile food bowl for growing fruit, vegetables and rice, with plentiful river fish and seafood from the coast.

At its heart is Bangkok, a dynamic, exciting city that never sleeps, where East meets West and the Old World meets the New. All kinds of food are available here, from curries and noodles served at street stalls to Thai meals in

Fourteenth-century, 19-metre (62¼-feet) high bronze Buddha in Wat Phanan Choeng, Ayuthaya.

family-run restaurants and all manner of fine dining opportunities in international five-star hotels. Trends may stray away from traditional presentation but Thais are very good at combining new ideas with existing concepts and love to experiment, so there's always somewhere new and fashionable to try out.

The newest restaurant at the Peninsula Bangkok, The Thipt, is Thai. The latest in world food is being served in restaurants such as 87 at the Conrad Hotel on Wireless Road, while The Oriental Bangkok is the world-famous hotel which has welcomed royalty and discerning travellers for more than 120 years and has helped to put Thai food on the map with its cooking schools.

Heavily influenced by the cuisine of the Royal Palace, dishes from the Central region have traditionally been created to appeal to all the senses, with the visual aspect playing an extremely important part in presentation. Intricate carving of fruits and vegetables and the use of flowers typifies the revered Palace "look". It was King Rama IV who introduced the knife and spoon to Thailand where previously hands had been used – chopsticks have never been used in Thailand except in Chinese restaurants or when eating Chinese noodle dishes.

In Bangkok the Sky Train is a fantastic way to speed across the city while seeing the Royal Palace and temples, such as Wat Arun. Less than 100 kilometres (62 miles) north of Bangkok is Ayuthaya, formerly the capital city. Some of its temples have been restored and there are night markets and some floating restaurants. South of Bangkok, the Hua Hin Peninsula is a revered strip of land which is home to royal summer palaces and hotels. Eating seafood on the jetty at Hua Hin is a further unforgettable experience.

Gluay khai *bananas on sale at Damnoen Saduak floating market near Bangkok.*

hot and sour fish soup with tamarind and coriander

Tom khlong

Hot and sour are two of the basic flavours of Thai cooking, and distinctive tamarind and tangy lemon provide the sour base for this delicious soup. Dried fish is traditionally used, which you can find in Asian grocery shops, or use fresh fish as I have done here.

5 shallots, chopped and crushed

6 dried chillies, deseeded and
  soaked in warm water

300 g (10 oz) fish fillets, such as
  cod, or shelled and deveined
  raw prawns

700 ml (1¼ pints) Fish Stock (see
  page 138)

1 lemongrass stalk, finely sliced

4 slices of galangal

2 tablespoons Tamarind Juice
  (see pages 16–17)

¾ tablespoon fresh lime juice

3½ tablespoons fish sauce

4 whole coriander leaves, to
  garnish

Preheat the oven to 160°C (325°F) Gas Mark 3. Wrap the crushed shallots and dried chillies in foil to make a sealed parcel. Rinse and pat dry the fish fillets or prawns and put on to a baking tray. Put both the foil parcel and the fish into the oven and cook for 10 minutes.

Remove both items from the oven. Cut the fish into bite-sized pieces, discarding any bones.

Bring the stock to the boil then add the lemongrass, baked shallots, baked dried chillies, galangal and fish and simmer for 10 minutes, until the fish is cooked. Skim off the soup and season with the tamarind juice, lime juice and fish sauce to obtain a sour and salty taste. Add the coriander leaves, and serve.

Hot
Serves 4 as part of a Thai meal
Preparation and cooking time: 40 minutes

Fresh tamarind and young leaves are used to add an important "sour" taste to Thai dishes.

king prawn soup with chilli and lime

Tom yum goong

This classic soup is hot and spicy, sour and aromatic all at the same time. For many people around the world who love Thai food *Tom Yum Goong* soup is a measure of the quality of the chef, and many people swear by this soup to clear their heads when they have a cold!

1 L (1¾ pt) Fish Stock (see page 138)

1 lemongrass stalk, sliced into rings

4 slices of galangal

4 kaffir lime leaves, torn

1½ tablespoons Roasted Chilli Paste (see page 14)

4 hot chillies, or to taste

8 straw or button mushrooms, quartered

8 raw king prawns, shelled and deveined

4 tablespoons fresh lime juice

4½ tablespoons fish sauce

1 tablespoon chopped coriander

1 tablespoon finely sliced spring onion

8 coriander leaves, to garnish

Bring the stock to the boil in a large pan or stockpot, add the lemongrass, galangal, kaffir lime leaves and roasted chilli paste and simmer for about 20 minutes.

Increase the heat and bring to the boil, add the chilli and mushrooms and bring back to the boil. Add the king prawns, cook for 2 minutes then add the lime juice, fish sauce, chopped coriander and spring onion. Stir together briefly and serve garnished with coriander leaves.

Hot
Serves 4 as part of a Thai meal
Preparation and cooking time: 40 minutes

Fresh king prawns this size (approx. 200 grammes/7 ounces) are available all-year-round.

chicken and coconut soup
Tom kha gai

This dish balances the sweetness of coconut milk and the fragrance of galangal, kaffir lime leaves and lemongrass, with the salty fish sauce and the sour taste of lime juice. The fried chillies add a smoky flavour as well as texture, colour and heat, but not so much that it overwhelms the soup.

500 ml (18 fl oz) Chicken Stock
  (see page 138)
4 kaffir lime leaves, torn in half
1 lemongrass stalk, crushed
12 thin slices of galangal
300 g (10 oz) chicken breasts,
  thinly sliced
500 ml (18 fl oz) Coconut Milk
  (see page 16)
60 g (2 oz) straw mushrooms (or
  button or field mushrooms)
4 tablespoons fresh lime juice
4½ tablespoons fish sauce
8 small crispy-fried chillies
8 coriander leaves, to garnish

Heat the chicken stock in a large, deep pan then add the lime leaves, lemongrass and galangal. Simmer for 10 minutes then add the chicken and coconut milk and bring to the boil.

Add the mushrooms, lime juice and fish sauce to the pan and bubble, uncovered, until the chicken is cooked, about 20 minutes. Add the fried chillies to the soup and serve immediately, garnished with coriander leaves.

Medium-hot
Serves 4 as part of a Thai meal
Preparation and cooking time: 25 minutes

Monkeys are trained to collect coconuts – young or old coconuts are selected according to the trainer's call.

banana flower salad

yum hau pee

This is a wonderful Thai dish which combines the deliciously rich and creamy flavour of the banana flower with crunchy cashews nuts, the heat of the roasted chilli and all the other ingredients. Banana flowers are actually the buds of the banana plant, which are soaked and shredded for use in salads. They are also available preserved from Asian grocery shops – soak in cold water for 10 minutes and rinse before using.

1 L (1¾ pt) cold water
100 g (3½ oz) skinless, boneless
  chicken breast, sliced
100 g (3½oz) raw king prawns,
  shelled and deveined
1 banana flower, weighing
  about 200 g (7 oz)
2 tablespoons fresh lime juice
50 g (2 oz) dried shrimps, finely
  chopped
1 tablespoon sliced shallots
2 tablespoons roasted cashew
  nuts, crushed
8 crispy-fried chillies
1 shallot, sliced and fried
Handful of coriander leaves and
  3 pieces of banana flower, to
  garnish

DRESSING
2½ tablespoons fish sauce
3 tablespoons fresh lime juice
½ tablespoon palm sugar
1½ tablespoons Roasted Chilli
  Paste (see page 14)
¼ teaspoon dried, roasted chilli
  powder
3 tablespoons Coconut Milk (see
  page 16)

Bring 500 ml (18 fl oz) of water to the boil in a saucepan then add the chicken pieces, reduce to a simmer and cook for 5 minutes. Add the prawns and continue simmering for 3 minutes, until cooked. Remove the chicken and the prawns and set aside. Discard water.

Remove and discard all the hard leaves from the banana flower, then thinly slice the white inside part diagonally. Mix the lime juice with 500 ml (18 fl oz) of cold water and soak the banana flower slices for 5 minutes to prevent discoloration.

Make the dressing. In a bowl combine the fish sauce, lime juice, palm sugar, chilli paste, chilli powder and coconut milk. Mix them together well until the palm sugar has completely dissolved.

Gently squeeze the water from the banana flower and then combine it with the dressing, the chicken and prawns, dried shrimps, tablespoon of sliced shallots and cashew nuts. Mix well then serve sprinkled with the crispy-fried chillies and fried shallots and garnish with coriander leaves and banana flower pieces.

Medium-hot
Serves 4 as part of a Thai meal
Preparation and cooking time: 1 hour

jungle chicken curry
gaeng pa gai

This aromatic and highly spiced curry is one of the five hottest dishes in Thailand, traditionally made with anything and everything available in the jungle! My grandfather loved to eat this once a week, believing that it was good for the digestion and that it kept the flu away – a tradition he continued until his death at the ripe old age of 95.

1 tablespoon Red Curry Paste
 (see page 15)
1 tablespoon chopped garlic
1 tablespoon chopped red chilli
1 tablespoon vegetable oil
1 tablespoon lesser ginger
3 stalks green peppercorns,
 fresh or preserved
200 g (7 oz) chicken breast
fillets, sliced
350 ml (13 fl oz) Chicken Stock
 (see page 138)
4 kaffir lime leaves
50 g (1½ oz) sliced bamboo
 shoots
4 pieces of baby corn (other
 vegetables can be added too,
 such as broccoli and carrots)
30 g (1 oz) wood or cloud ear
 mushrooms (or use field
 mushrooms)
Handful of holy basil
3 teaspoons fish sauce
1 teaspoon palm sugar

Using a pestle and mortar, pound the red curry paste together with the garlic and chilli until fine. Heat a heavy-bottomed saucepan, add the oil and the pounded paste and fry, stirring together until the paste turns light brown.

Add the lesser ginger and peppercorns and stir-fry for 2 minutes, until fragrant, then add the chicken and cook for a further 2 minutes. Now pour in the stock, add the Kaffir lime leaves and bring to the boil. Add the bamboo shoots, baby corn (and any other vegetables), mushrooms, holy basil, fish sauce and palm sugar. Cook for a further 5 minutes.

Very hot
Serves 4 as part of a Thai meal
Preparation and cooking time: 20 minutes

Fresh krachai *(lesser ginger) on sale at a petrol station's stall.*

green chicken curry
gaeng khiao wan gai

A favourite dish in Thai restaurants around the world, *gaeng khiao wan gai* means "green sweet curry", the sweetness deriving from the coconut milk and palm sugar. It is also deliciously hot and aromatic thanks to the green chilli, peppercorns, kaffir lime leaves and sweet basil, and salty through the shrimp paste and fish sauce.

200 ml (7 fl oz) coconut cream,
  plus 1 tablespoon to garnish
1 tablespoon Green Curry
  Paste (see page 15)
4 kaffir lime leaves, torn
300 g (10 oz) chicken breast
  fillets, sliced
4 tablespoons fish sauce
2 teaspoons palm sugar
400 ml (13 fl oz) Coconut Milk
  (see page 16)
3 Thai aubergines, quartered (or
  green beans or fresh green
  peas)
2 long red chillies, sliced
  diagonally
Handful of Thai sweet basil
  (reserve a few leaves to
  garnish)

Heat the coconut cream in a medium saucepan over a low heat. Add the green curry paste and stir, cooking for about 4–5 minutes until the green curry paste oil separates and rises to the surface.

Add the kaffir lime leaves and the chicken slices to the pan. Cook, stirring, for 2 minutes then add the fish sauce, palm sugar, coconut milk and the Thai aubergines. Boil (uncovered) for a further 7 minutes until the chicken is cooked, stirring often to prevent sticking and burning.

Add the sliced chillies and basil, stirring together for about 1 minute. Serve the curry in a bowl, garnished with 1 tablespoon of coconut cream and the reserved basil leaves.

Hot
Serves 4 as part of a Thai meal
Preparation and cooking time: 30 minutes

Traditional home beside a klong *(canal) in Central Thailand.*

red duck curry with pineapple

gaeng ped pet yang kai khem

The use of pineapple in this recipe is an example of the Thai tradition of balancing flavours, adding sweetness to offset the richness of the duck. Very old recipes include salty eggs, which are made by preserving fresh, uncooked duck eggs in a brine solution for three weeks or longer. Salty eggs are available from Asian grocers if you wish to include one, stirring in over the heat just before serving.

400 g (13½ oz) roasted duck
  meat
100 ml (4 fl oz) coconut cream
2 tablespoons Red Curry Paste
  (see page 15)
400 ml (13 fl oz) Coconut Milk
  (see page 16)
5 kaffir lime leaves, finely sliced
3½ tablespoons fish sauce
4 teaspoons palm sugar
8 cherry tomatoes
3 long red chillies, sliced
100 g (3½ oz) fresh pineapple,
  cut into chunks
Handful of Thai sweet basil
Rice, to serve

Slice the cooked duck into roughly 3-cm (about 1-in) long pieces. Heat the coconut cream in a saucepan over a medium heat, add the red curry paste and stir for about 7–10 minutes, until the curry paste oil separates and rises to the surface. Stir well. Reserve 1 teaspoon of the coconut milk for garnish and slowly add the remainder to the pan.

Add the kaffir lime leaves and stir over a low heat for about 5 minutes then add the fish sauce and the palm sugar and cook until the oil again rises to the surface. Now add the duck pieces, cherry tomatoes, chillies and pineapple chunks. Reserve two or three Thai basil leaves for garnish and add the remainder to the pan. Boil together for 3 minutes then garnish with the reserved coconut milk and basil leaves and serve with plain rice.

Medium-hot
Serves 4 as part of a Thai meal
Preparation and cooking time: 30 minutes

stir-fried lamb with holy basil

lamb pad krapao

Holy basil is a classic ingredient in Thai stir-fry dishes made with prawns, pork and here with lamb. Thais like nothing better than to serve the *pad krapao* with fried egg, rice and fish sauce with slices of hot chilli.

2 tablespoons vegetable oil

1 tablespoon finely chopped garlic

1 teaspoon chopped small red chillies

Handful of holy basil

300 g (10 oz) lamb fillets, sliced into 7-cm (3-in) pieces

½ onion, finely sliced

1 tablespoon soy sauce

1 tablespoon fish sauce

1 tablespoon oyster sauce

1 teaspoon caster sugar

2 long red chillies, sliced

2 spring onions, cut into 5-cm (2-in) pieces

Handful of crispy-fried Thai sweet basil

Heat the oil in a wok until it smokes then add the garlic, chopped chilli and holy basil. Quickly stir-fry for about 10–15 seconds, until fragrant.

Add the lamb pieces and stir-fry until sealed, then add the onion, soy sauce, fish sauce, oyster sauce and sugar. Cook, stirring constantly, until the meat is medium rare – sealed on the outside but still pink and juicy inside.

Add the sliced red chillies and spring onion to the wok, stir to mix and serve immediately, garnished with the crispy-fried Thai sweet basil.

Hot
Serves 4 as part of a Thai meal
Preparation and cooking time: 20 minutes

Modern equipment plus traditional people power speeds the rice harvest.

panang beef

gaeng panang nue

This recipe is usually made with beef but regular customers of the Arun Thai restaurant in Sydney have also grown to love our chicken version. You can also use prawns or other seafood, or pork. This very traditional Thai curry is thicker than most because of the mung beans in the Panang curry paste which help to create the deliciously thick sauce.

100 ml (4 fl oz) coconut cream
1 tablespoon Panang Curry
  Paste (see page 15)
400 g (14 oz) beef, sirloin or
  topside, sliced
350 ml (11 fl oz) Coconut Milk
  (see page 16)
3 kaffir lime leaves
3 tablespoons fish sauce
1 teaspoon palm sugar
1 small red chilli, sliced
Handful of Thai sweet basil

Heat the coconut cream in a heavy-bottomed saucepan over a medium heat, add the curry paste and stir until the paste oil separates and rises to the surface.

Stir in the beef, mixing well with the coconut cream mixture. Reserve 1 tablespoon of the coconut milk for garnish and add the remainder to the pan, together with two of the kaffir lime leaves, roughly torn. Simmer for 10 minutes, stirring often, then blend in the fish sauce, palm sugar and simmer for a further 5 minutes until the beef is cooked and the curry has thickened.

Serve garnished with the reserved tablespoon of coconut milk, sliced chilli, the remaining kaffir lime leaf, finely sliced and a handful of Thai sweet basil leaves.

Medium-hot
Serves 4 as part of a Thai meal
Preparation and cooking time: 30 minutes

Detail from the beautiful Wat Arun in Bangkok.

steamed salmon in young coconut

hor mok pla

Traditional *hor mok* is a steamed red curry made with fish, chicken or seafood, wrapped in a banana leaf, but this dish can also be steamed in a whole young coconut for a toasty, aromatic flavour as well as a delicious taste. You need a deep steamer large enough to accommodate the coconut. If you can't source a young coconut you can also steam the mixture in foil, which will take about 25 minutes.

1 fresh green coconut

80 g (2½ oz) white fish fillets, such as sole or whiting, sliced

1 tablespoon Red Curry Paste (see page 15)

230 ml (8 fl oz) coconut cream

1 egg, beaten

1 tablespoon lesser ginger

3 kaffir lime leaves, finely sliced

1½ tablespoons fish sauce

1½ teaspoons caster sugar

100 g (3½ oz) salmon fillets, sliced

½ teaspoon ground white pepper

12 Thai sweet basil leaves

50 g (1½ oz) Chinese cabbage, steamed

Coconut Milk (see page 16) and 2 sliced red chillies, to serve

Partially slice the top off the coconut, leaving a hinge attached to form a lid. Drain off the coconut juice and leave the coconut upside down to drain, then wipe it dry inside.

In a blender, combine the white fish and red curry paste and blend until smooth, about 5 minutes. Pour the coconut cream into a large mixing bowl, add the blended fish, egg, lesser ginger, two of the sliced kaffir lime leaves, fish sauce, sugar, salmon fillets and white pepper and stir gently together in one direction only, in order to combine the ingredients without breaking them up. The mixture should then stick together.

Place the Thai sweet basil leaves and steamed Chinese cabbage at the bottom of the coconut, then top with the fish mixture. Close the lid of the coconut and place upright in a steamer to steam for 40 minutes. Alternatively, steam in a foil parcel for 25 minutes.

Serve garnished with the coconut milk, sliced chillies and the remaining sliced kaffir lime leaf.

Medium-hot
Serves 4 as part of a Thai meal
Preparation and cooking time: 1 hour 25 minutes

steamed fish with lime juice and chilli

pla neung manao

The coastline, rivers, canals and even the rice paddy fields of Thailand teem with fish, and many Thai people simply catch or net their own when it is time for the next meal. Select the freshest fish for this recipe. The cabbage leaves prevent the fish from sticking while it cooks.

600 g (1 lb 5 oz) firm white fish fillets, such as cod or haddock

Chinese cabbage or white cabbage leaves

Handful of Thai sweet basil leaves

2 tablespoons sliced lemongrass

2 teaspoons finely chopped coriander and 2 whole coriander leaves, to garnish

3 slices of lime (or lemon), to garnish

Rice and stir-fried vegetables, to serve

SAUCE
5 hot red chillies
3 garlic cloves
2 tablespoons fish sauce
3 tablespoons fresh lime juice
1 teaspoon caster sugar

Rinse the fish fillets, pat them dry and, using a sharp knife, carefully score about three times on each side.

Line a medium-sized plate with the cabbage leaves, sprinkle over the Thai sweet basil leaves and sliced lemongrass and lay the fish fillets on top. Place the plate in a steamer, cover and steam over boiling water for 15 minutes.

To make the sauce, chop the chillies and garlic cloves and combine in a bowl with the fish sauce, lime juice and sugar, mixing well until the sugar dissolves.

When the fish is ready remove the plate from the steamer, drain off the juices and transfer to a serving dish. Spoon over the sauce and sprinkle with the finely chopped coriander. Garnish with the whole coriander leaves and lime slices and serve with plain rice and some colourful stir-fried vegetables.

Very hot
Serves 4 as part of a Thai meal
Preparation and cooking time: 20 minutes

pan-fried salmon with chu chee curry sauce

chu chee pla salmon

Chu chee is a traditional curry sauce for seafood, such as prawns and scallops. Here I have combined it with salmon because the strong flavour, colour and texture of the fish goes particularly well with this rich red curry sauce.

CHU CHEE SAUCE
100 ml (3¼ fl oz) coconut cream
½ tablespoon Red Curry Paste
 (see page 15)
½ tablespoon Panang Curry
 Paste (see page 15)
200 ml (7 fl oz) Coconut Milk
 (see page 16)
2 tablespoons fish sauce
2 teaspoons palm sugar
100 ml (3¼ fl oz) vegetable oil

400 g (13½ oz) salmon fillets
5 Thai sweet basil leaves
1 kaffir lime leaf, finely sliced
1 hot red chilli, finely sliced

First make the sauce. Gently heat the coconut cream in a medium saucepan and add the curry pastes. Cook, stirring, for about 5 minutes, until the curry paste oil separates and rises to the surface. Add the coconut milk, fish sauce and palm sugar and simmer for 7 minutes, stirring often. Set aside and keep warm.

Heat the oil in a frying pan and fry the salmon until golden brown. Remove the salmon and add to the warm *Chu Chee sauce*, shaking gently to coat the salmon. Transfer the salmon and sauce to a serving dish and garnish with basil leaves, kaffir lime leaves and sliced chilli.

Medium-hot
Serves 4 as part of a Thai meal
Preparation and cooking time: 30 minutes

Buying snacks from a street stall to take home to the children.

stir-fried clams with chilli and basil

hoi lai pad horapha

Stir-fried shellfish is quick and easy to cook. This is a delicious way to serve clams or mussels, with hot chilli, soy sauce and basil. The important thing is to ensure that the wok is hot before you begin to add the ingredients.

500 g (13½ oz) fresh clams (or mussels), in the shell
2 tablespoons vegetable oil
1 small red chilli, finely chopped
1 teaspoon finely chopped garlic
1 tablespoon Roasted Chilli Paste (see page 14)
¾ tablespoon fish sauce
¾ tablespoon oyster sauce
1 teaspoon caster sugar
1 tablespoon Fish Stock (see page 138)
Handful of Thai sweet basil leaves

Rinse the clams thoroughly and drain. Discard any that have not closed.

Heat the oil in a wok or frying pan and add the chilli and garlic. Stir-fry quickly until the garlic is golden-brown – less than 1 minute. Add the clams and stir them until they open. Discard any that do not open. Add the roasted chilli paste, fish sauce, oyster sauce and sugar and stir, then pour in the fish stock. Cover and cook for 3 minutes. Add the basil, stir briefly and serve immediately.

Medium-hot
Serves 4 as part of a Thai meal
Preparation and cooking time: 25 minutes

Mobile juice sellers quench the thirst of Bangkok's busy workers.

stir-fried scampi with krachai and peppercorns

pad char scampi

This deliciously spicy dish is made without coconut milk. For the very best results the *Pad Char* paste should be freshly made – there are quite a few ingredients but it doesn't take long to combine them into an exquisitely fragrant paste! Fresh lesser ginger (*krachai*) is best, but not always widely available, so find the pickled variety in jars and rinse well in cold water before using.

PAD CHAR PASTE

8–10 slices red chilli

3 shallots, peeled and sliced

3 garlic cloves, peeled and chopped

1 lemongrass stalk, finely chopped

1 tablespoon finely chopped galangal

1 tablespoon chopped lesser ginger

2 kaffir lime leaves

4 stalks of green peppercorns, fresh or preserved

3 tablespoons vegetable oil

12 raw scampi (or king prawns), shelled, deveined and halved

3 tablespoons Chicken Stock (see page 138)

1½ tablespoons fish sauce

1 tablespoon oyster sauce

1 tablespoon soy sauce

2 teaspoons caster sugar

100 g (3½ oz) green beans

Handful of Thai sweet basil leaves

Handful of holy basil leaves

To make the paste pound the chilli and shallots using a pestle and mortar until fine, then transfer to a hot, dry wok with the garlic, lemongrass, galangal, lesser ginger, kaffir lime leaves and green peppercorns. Fry over a gentle heat for about 1 minute, until everything is well mixed and fragrant. You will know the paste is ready the moment you begin to smell the wonderful aroma. Remove the wok from the heat, transfer the paste to a bowl and set aside.

Add the oil to the wok and heat until it smokes. Add the *Pad Char* paste, stirring for 2 minutes, then add the scampi. Stir well and add the chicken stock, fish sauce, oyster sauce, soy sauce, sugar and green beans. Cover with a lid and bubble for 1 minute, then add the basil leaves, toss through and serve immediately.

Hot
Serves 4 as part of a Thai meal
Preparation and cooking time: 30 minutes

Fishing boats at Rayong catch anchovies – the main ingredient for making fish sauce – each day.

stir-fried crab with yellow curry sauce

pu pad pong khari

This combines Chinese stir-fry and Indian curry influences with two very important Thai ingredients – chilli and garlic. Preparing crab can be rather fiddly, but it is well worth the effort. Shelled raw prawns can be used instead of the crab, if preferred.

1 fresh uncooked crab,
  weighing about 500 g
  (1 lb 2 oz)
4 red chillies
2 garlic cloves, peeled
2 tablespoons vegetable oil
100 ml (4 fl oz) milk
1 egg
1 tablespoon soy sauce
1 tablespoon oyster sauce
2 teaspoons caster sugar
1 teaspoon ground white
  pepper
2 teaspoons medium to hot
  curry powder
80 g (2½ oz) sliced onion
80 g (2½ oz) chopped spring
  onions

Wash the crab, remove the shell and claw then chop the crab into six pieces using a cleaver. Using the back of the cleaver, lightly crack the claws to make them easy to open.

Pound two of the chillies and garlic together using a pestle and mortar. Heat the oil in a wok, add the pounded chilli and garlic and stir for about 1 minute. Slice the remaining chillies and add to the wok. Add the crab and stir for about 8 minutes, until it turns pink.

Beat the milk and egg together in a bowl and add to the crab, cooking for 2–3 minutes, then add the soy sauce, oyster sauce, sugar, pepper and curry powder, stirring well to mix. Add the sliced onion and chopped spring onions. Cover with a lid and cook for about 2 minutes until the sauce thickens, then check that the crab is cooked, using the tip of a knife to part the flesh of the largest chunks. Cooked crab meat is white. Transfer to a serving plate, arrange and serve.

Medium-hot
Serves 4 as part of a Thai meal
Preparation and cooking time: 30 minutes

Crabs from Southern Thailand are available all-year-round and are favourites in the Central and Northern regions of the country.

stir-fried rice noodles with king prawns

pad thai goong

Noodles and stir-frying were introduced to Thailand by Chinese immigrants and both fitted easily into Thai cooking principles because they were quick to prepare and very tasty. *Pad thai* (stir-fried Thai noodles) are widely available from street stalls all over Thailand and are one of the most famous of all Thai dishes. They are particularly delicious with duck eggs.

200 g (7 oz) medium rice stick noodles

1½ tablespoons vegetable oil

2 teaspoons dried shrimps

8 raw king prawns, shelled and deveined

2 eggs (use duck eggs if you like)

3 tablespoons cubed firm tofu (beancurd)

1 tablespoon pickled radish (optional)

5 teaspoons caster sugar

2 tablespoons fish sauce

3 tablespoons Tamarind Juice (see pages 16–17)

2 teaspoons chilli powder, or to taste

80 g (2½ oz) beansprouts

10 Chinese chives, chopped into 7.5-cm (3-in) lengths

2 tablespoons ground roasted peanuts

1 lime, quartered

Banana blossom

Soak the rice noodles in warm water for 15 minutes, then remove and drain.

Heat the oil in a wok, add the dried shrimps and cook until golden-brown. Add the king prawns and stir until cooked, about 2 minutes, then add the eggs, tofu, pickled radish, rice noodles, sugar, fish sauce, tamarind juice, 1 teaspoon of the chilli powder and half the beansprouts and stir well until the noodles are cooked.

Add half the chives and stir. Serve garnished with the remaining beansprouts and chives, ground roasted peanuts, lime wedges and a banana blossom if possible. Offer the second teaspoon of chilli powder in a little pile so that it can be stirred in to taste.

Spicy
Serves 4 as part of a Thai meal
Preparation and cooking time: 25 minutes

roasted tofu with chilli, coriander and mushrooms

Taohu ob

Good for a healthy diet, tofu (beancurd) has been eaten in northern Asia for many thousands of years. Following its introduction, it soon became a very popular ingredient in Thai cuisine. The silken tofu used in this recipe is good for roasting and for soups – here it is placed over the other ingredients and the pan is shaken, not stirred, to avoid breaking up the tofu.

1 tablespoon vegetable oil
30 g (1 oz) root ginger, sliced
  into fine strips
1 small red chilli, crushed
2 garlic cloves, crushed
2 coriander roots, crushed
½ teaspoon ground white
  pepper
1½ tablespoons oyster sauce
1½ tablespoons soy sauce
1 teaspoon caster sugar
500 g (1 lb 2 oz) silken tofu
  (beancurd)
250 ml (8 fl oz) Vegetable Stock
  (see page 138)
3 spring onions, cut into 7-cm
  (3-in) pieces
50 g (1½ oz) brown, oyster,
  shiitake or *hed kon* (wild)
  mushrooms, finely sliced
Whole coriander leaves and a
  few slices of chilli, to garnish

Heat the oil in a deep saucepan with the ginger, chilli, garlic, coriander, pepper, oyster sauce, soy sauce and sugar and place the tofu on top. Pour in the vegetable stock, cover with a lid and cook for about 7 minutes to reduce the liquid, occasionally shaking the pan to prevent sticking.

Remove the lid and add the spring onions and mushrooms and cook, covered, for a further 2 minutes. Garnish with coriander leaves and chilli slices and serve immediately.

Medium-hot
Serves 4 as part of a Thai meal
Preparation and cooking time: 25 minutes

A great delicacy, hed kon *mushrooms grow on old timbers when the rains come.*

crispy fish salad
with green mango

yum pla duk foo

In Thailand this would be made with catfish, a tasty river fish that is popular throughout Asia as its texture is perfect for frying until crisp. To make this recipe, choose a fine-textured rather than a flaky fish to make it easier to fry. Green apple can be substituted for green mango. Serve the salad at room temperature, or cold.

200 g (7 oz) catfish or other
  white fish fillets
500 ml (18 fl oz) vegetable oil
10 g (¼ oz) plain flour
100 g (4 oz) grated green
  mango or green apple
3 tablespoons cashew nuts
Coriander leaves, to garnish

SAUCE
2½ tablespoons fish sauce
2 tablespoons fresh lime juice
2 teaspoons palm sugar
2 shallots, peeled and sliced
1 red chilli, sliced

Steam the fish fillets in a steamer for about 10 minutes. Remove from the heat, pat dry with kitchen paper and use a fork to break the fillets into pieces. Heat the oil in a medium, heavy-based frying pan, deep enough for the oil to cover the fish.

Coat the fish pieces in the flour and deep-fry until golden brown. Remove the fish from the oil and drain on kitchen paper. Transfer the fish pieces to a serving plate and top with grated green mango.

To make the sauce put the fish sauce, lime juice and palm sugar in a bowl and stir until the sugar has dissolved, then add the shallots and chilli. Mix well and pour over the fish and mango salad. Scatter over the cashew nuts and coriander leaves and serve.

Medium-hot
Serves 4 as part of a Thai meal
Preparation and cooking time: 30 minutes

Green mangoes piled high in the markets.

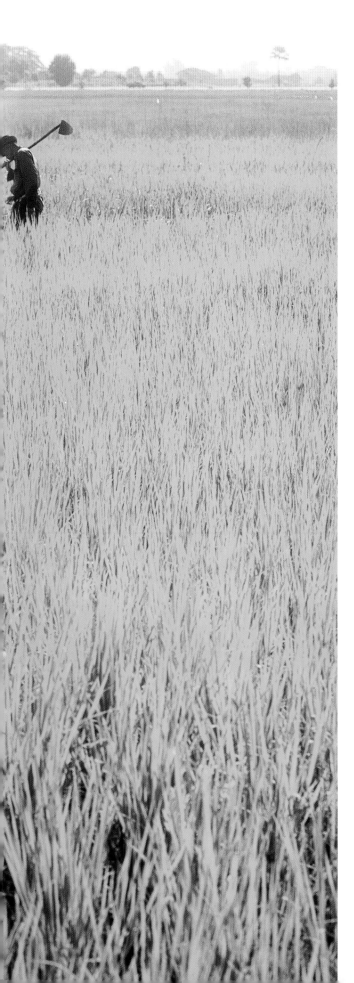

Isan – the Northeast

Fresh herbs & hot chilli

I was brought up beside the Mekong River, and spent a great deal of time on it and in it. I am Thai, although my birthplace was Savannakhet on the Laos side, but we didn't think of the two sides as different countries at all as the water was like a highway to us. After school, my friends and I would swim the 1½ kilometres (1 mile) across this famous river to play with children on the Mukdahan (Thai) side and when we weren't swimming it we were crisscrossing it at great speed in the longtail water taxis.

Sharing the long Mekong River, Isan has more similarities with Laos than with the other regions of Thailand. In the Northeast of the region people speak Lao and are referred to as Lao by other Thais. Further south Khmer is spoken in the areas bordering Cambodia. All through Isan you can see the influences in the shared architecture of the temples as well as in the food.

Isan food is very fresh and uncomplicated, known for its robust flavours. The northeast is not a fertile region as the hot dry season is followed by rains that cause flooding, so the friendly people here are used to tough conditions and to making do with whatever food is available. Despite this, feasts are much enjoyed here, with blessings from the monks and the elders to celebrate weddings and special occasions.

Sticky rice is a Thai staple, used a bit like bread, and the Isan tradition is to eat with the hands, dipping balls of sticky rice into sauces and curry dishes. Our salads (*larb*)

Farmer working in the rice fields after the welcome rainy season in Isan.

are served Laotian-style but ingredients such as duck and fish are chopped rather than minced as they are in Laos and mixed with fresh mint, spring onions, chillies, lime juice and ground roasted rice.

I was lucky to be brought up so close to the river, where plenty of fish was available – Thais love fresh fish of any description. Isan is infamous for *pla ra*, an extremely strong-smelling fermented fish, which is served with sticky rice. Bottled fish sauce is also widely used.

The region is generally poor but what dishes lack in the refinement of the coconut milk and spices of the South, they make up for in the heat of chillies and fresh tastes of mint, spring onion, coriander, lime and lemon basil. Special Isan dishes include Crying Tiger (see pages 78–79), grilled beef served with a fresh, hot spicy sauce, spicy salads, Waterfall Beef Salad (see pages 68–69), Isan Mushroom Salad (see pages 70–71) and the famous Spicy Papaya Salad (see pages 66–67), which is loved throughout Thailand. All the Isan dishes go perfectly with sticky rice.

Recently on a visit to Isan I noticed that times have really changed – the airport is bigger and the road from the Southern and Central region is much faster now. For cooking, the variety of ingredients is much wider but the basic ingredients for Isan cooking are still the same. Two things I was thrilled to eat again for the first time in many years were *yum hed kon*, a very rare mushroom with a sweet, exotic taste found only during the rainy season growing on the nest of the white ant. I was enjoying these in a restaurant in Nong Khai when I also saw a street vendor pass by with a basket full of fresh lotus seeds and I had to run after her and buy some. With all the delicacy of rose petals, their flavour is exquisite.

The Mekong River divides Thailand and Laos, but the culture as well as the dialect and food is very similar on both sides of the river.

isan sour fish soup
gaeng som pla isan

Isan soups are clear and clean-tasting, very different to the chilli paste-based *tom yum* soups of the Central region. Any white fish is suitable for this soup, such as cod or monkfish. The stock for the soup must be boiling before you add the fish or the fishy taste will be overpowering. If you prefer less heat, use only one or two chillies.

8 slices galangal

2– 4 hot chillies, to taste

4 cloves garlic, chopped

2 shallots, sliced

1 lemongrass stalk, cut into
   5-cm (2-in) pieces

1 L (1¾ pt) Fish Stock (see
   page 138)

4 kaffir lime leaves, torn

500 g (1 lb 2 oz) white fish
   fillets, sliced into 5-cm (2-in)
   pieces

8 cherry tomatoes

4 tablespoons Tamarind Juice
   (see pages 16–17)

3½ tablespoons fish sauce

1 tablespoon fresh lime juice

100 g (3½ oz) straw mushrooms

1 tablespoon finely chopped
   coriander

1 spring onion, cut into 5-cm
   (2-in) pieces

2 sprigs of dill

Using a pestle and mortar, pound the galangal, chillies, garlic, shallots and lemongrass until fine.

Heat 300 ml (10 fl oz) of the fish stock in a saucepan then add the pounded ingredients and the torn kaffir lime leaves. Bring to the boil then reduce the heat and simmer for 10 minutes to aromatize.

Add the remaining fish stock and bring to the boil once more then add the fish fillets. Cook for about 8 minutes, until the fish is done. Add the cherry tomatoes and season with the tamarind juice, fish sauce and lime juice, then drop in the mushrooms and continue to cook for about 2 minutes. Serve the soup hot, sprinkled with coriander and chopped spring onion. Garnish with dill sprigs.

Hot
Serves 4 as part of a Thai meal
Preparation and cooking time: 30 minutes

Mekong ferry boats carry passengers and goods of all kinds between towns and villages in Laos and Thailand.

isan duck salad
larb pet isan

One of the great Thai classics, originally from the eastern part of Thailand, this dish combines meat and herbs with lime juice for an explosion of irresistible, spicy, fresh tastes. This goes well with sticky rice and is perfectly balanced by the coolness of the lettuce and cucumber.

300 g (10 oz) fresh duck breasts
  (or use ready-roasted duck)
4 slices galangal
4 tablespoons fresh lime juice
2 teaspoons caster sugar
3 tablespoons fish sauce
1 shallot, finely sliced
½ teaspoon chilli powder
Handful of mint leaves
1 tablespoon ground rice
1 spring onion, chopped
2 lemongrass stalks, finely sliced
1 tablespoon chopped coriander
Lettuce leaves, cucumber slices,
  green beans, crispy-fried
  chillies and whole, fresh
  chillies, to serve

If using fresh duck, grill the breasts for about 7 minutes each side. Wrap the galangal in foil and grill for 5 minutes. When this is done, chop the duck and the galangal into fine slices.

Mix the lime juice, sugar and fish sauce in a bowl until the sugar dissolves, then add the duck and galangal mixture, shallot, chilli powder, mint, ground rice, spring onion, lemongrass and coriander and mix well, so all the flavours are combined. Serve with lettuce, cucumber slices, green beans, crispy-fried chillies and fresh chillies on the side.

Hot
Serves 4 as part of a Thai meal
Preparation and cooking time: 40 minutes

Hungry Isan people wait for freshly-cooked food at house-front stalls.

papaya salad
with barbecued chicken

som Tum gai yang

Huge quantities of this are consumed every day in Thailand so it is very much a national dish. Tomato and papaya are used all over the country but the Thai people in the Northeast traditionally use fermented fish and fermented crabs in addition to fish sauce.

1 fresh chicken, weighing 1.2 kg
(2 lb 12 oz)

MARINADE
2 garlic cloves
2 coriander roots
2 teaspoons caster sugar
2 tablespoons light soy sauce
½ teaspoon salt

PAPAYA SALAD
3 garlic cloves
3 bird's eye chillies
30 g (1 oz) roasted peanuts
30 g (1 oz) dried shrimps
8 cherry tomatoes
3 tablespoons fish sauce
2 teaspoons palm sugar
4½ tablespoons fresh lime juice
250 g (8 oz) sliced green papaya
4 lettuce leaves
4 green beans, halved

Cut the chicken in half lengthways using poultry shears or ask your butcher to do this for you.

To make the marinade, put the garlic and coriander in a large bowl and pound together, then add the sugar, soy sauce and salt. Put the spatchcocked chicken on a plate and rub the mixture all over it, inside and out, then cover with clingfilm and leave in the fridge overnight.

When you are ready to eat, barbecue or grill the chicken for 15–20 minutes over a medium heat, then slice the meat off the bone.

Make the papaya salad. Using a pestle and mortar, pound the garlic, chillies, peanuts and dried shrimps to a fine paste. Mix the paste with the cherry tomatoes, fish sauce, palm sugar and lime juice. Mix well then add the green beans and papaya. Stir to mix without breaking up the papaya, then serve with the hot barbecued chicken and lettuce leaves on the side.

Hot
Serves 4 as part of a Thai meal
Preparation and cooking time: Overnight for marinating the chicken, 30 minutes for salad

waterfall beef salad
nue yang nam tok

In Northeastern Thailand beef is traditionally cooked over charcoal and it is the juices running off it that give this dish its name, which literally means "waterfall beef". The tender beef strips are spiked with spicy, pungent flavours and served with a cooling salad of cucumber, lettuce, mint and a little fresh chilli. The Thai way to eat this is with your hands, gathering up all the ingredients so you have a taste of everything in each bite.

300 g (10½ oz) piece sirloin or
  rump steak
3 tablespoons fish sauce
3½ tablespoons fresh lime juice
1 teaspoon palm sugar
1 tablespoon finely chopped
  coriander
2 spring onions, finely sliced
2 shallots, finely sliced
Handful of mint leaves
2 teaspoons ground rice
½ teaspoon chilli powder

SALAD
To taste, including lettuce
  leaves, sliced cucumber, sliced
  spring onions, coriander
  leaves, mint leaves, whole
  fresh chillies, to taste

Barbecue or grill the steak, ideally to medium-rare, and slice carefully into thin strips.

Mix the fish sauce, lime juice and palm sugar together in a bowl until the sugar has dissolved, then add the beef strips. Add the coriander, spring onions, shallots, mint leaves, ground rice and chilli powder and mix well.

To serve, assemble the salad on a plate and serve with the sliced beef.

Hot
Serves 4 as part of a Thai meal
Preparation and cooking time: 25 minutes

Sausages and meatballs on sale at the Isan markets.

isan mushroom salad

soop hed isan

In the Isan dialect *soop* actually means salad and this recipe, with a Lao influence, is a bowl of moist seasoned mushrooms to eat with sticky rice. In Thailand the shallots, chillies and garlic would be wrapped in banana leaves and cooked over a fire but grilling will help to achieve a degree of the smoky flavour.

200 g (7 oz) oyster mushrooms
  (or any white mushrooms)
1 shallot, unpeeled
1 or 2 small red chillies, to taste
2 garlic cloves, unpeeled
2 tablespoons fish sauce
2 tablespoons fresh lime juice
1 tablespoon caster sugar
1 spring onion, finely chopped
1 tablespoon finely chopped
  coriander
Lettuce, cucumber and Thai
  aubergines, to serve

Grill the mushrooms, shallot, chillies and garlic (all unpeeled) for about 6 minutes, until they change colour. Remove and leave to cool. When cool enough to handle, peel off the skin from the shallot and garlic, then, using a pestle and mortar, pound the flesh of the shallot, chillies and garlic until finely ground.

Mix the fish sauce, lime juice and sugar in a serving bowl until the sugar dissolves, then add the pounded shallot, chillies and garlic. Tear the mushrooms into strips and add them to the mixture together with the chopped spring onion and coriander. Stir and serve with lettuce, cucumber and Thai aubergines. Goes well with crispy-fried fish (shown opposite) and barbecued chicken or pork.

Hot
Serves 4 as part of a Thai meal
Preparation and cooking time: 20 minutes

Oyster mushrooms are widely used in Thai cooking and are available all over the world.

vegetable curry with venison

orm nue kuang

Orm means to simmer ingredients together in stock like a stew. The small native jungle deer from the Thai rainforests are nearly extinct, so today, as in many other countries, farmed venison is used.

1 red chilli, or to taste

1 lemongrass stalk, finely chopped

1 shallot, sliced

5 slices galangal

1 L (1¾ pt) Chicken Stock (see page 138)

400 g (14 oz) leg of venison, cut into thick strips or chunks

100 g (3½ oz) courgettes, chopped

100 g (3½ oz) green beans, cut into 2.5-cm (1-in) slices

50g (1½ oz) butternut squash, peeled and sliced into bite-sized pieces

2 Thai aubergines, quartered

4 tablespoons fish sauce

1 tablespoon caster sugar

2 spring onions, sliced into 2.5-cm (1-in) pieces

Handful of Thai sweet basil

Sprigs of dill, to garnish

Using a pestle and mortar, pound the chilli, lemongrass, shallot and galangal until fine.

Heat 250 ml (8 fl oz) of the chicken stock in a medium saucepan, add the pounded ingredients and cook until you can smell the fresh, tangy aroma. Now add the venison and the remaining chicken stock, cover and simmer for about 1 hour, until the venison is tender.

Add all the vegetables (except the spring onions) to the pan and cook until they are soft, then season with the fish sauce, sugar, spring onions and basil. Cook for a further 2 minutes then serve with plain rice. Garnish with sprigs of dill.

Medium-hot
Serves 4 as part of a Thai meal
Preparation and cooking time: 2 hours

Fresh produce, like these long beans, is available in the morning markets every day.

steamed chicken in banana leaves

hor mok gai

People from my region don't use much coconut milk for cooking, opting instead for ingredients such as basil, galangal, chilli and shallots, pounded together to form a paste which can be used as a marinade for chicken, fish, frogs' legs, vegetables or whatever is available on the day. As well as enclosing the chicken for cooking, the banana leaves add flavour. If you cannot find them use foil to wrap the chicken for steaming instead. Banana flowers preserved in salt and water are exported internationally from Thailand, and can be found in specialist shops. Soak them for 10 minutes then rinse to remove the salty taste.

1 lemongrass stalk, finely sliced

2 teaspoons galangal, finely chopped

2 shallots, finely sliced

5 red chillies, sliced

½ teaspoon salt

400 g (14 oz) skinless, boneless chicken breast, sliced into chunks

2 tablespoons fish sauce

1 teaspoon caster sugar

½ banana flower, soaked in water with 2 tablespoons fresh lime juice added to prevent discoloration

4 banana leaf pieces, cut into 15 x 15-cm (6 x 6-in) pieces

Handful of Thai basil leaves

Sliced chilli and 1 teaspoon Coconut Milk (see page 16), to garnish

Using a mortar and pestle, pound the sliced lemongrass, galangal, shallots, chillies and salt.

Transfer to a bowl and add the sliced chicken, fish sauce and sugar, stirring to mix well. Squeeze the water out of the banana flower and lay the flower on the banana leaf pieces, then the basil leaves and the chicken on top. Fold the leaves to form a parcel and seal with cocktail sticks. (If you use foil, wrap to create a parcel.) Steam for 20 minutes and serve. Garnish with sliced chilli and coconut milk.

Hot
Serves 4 as part of a Thai meal
Preparation and cooking time: 40 minutes

Family restaurants serving local food are open all day throughout Thailand.

steamed fish with vegetables and spicy sauce

pla nung jeew

Isan-style steamed fish has a clean, fresh taste, popular in the cooler weather when the temperature drops to 10°C (50°F), which is very cold by local standards. Use sole or any other firm, white fish suitable for steaming.

Steamed Vegetable and Fish
  Dipping Sauce (see pages
  138–139)
700 g (1 lb 9 oz) white fish
  fillets (or 1 whole fish, cleaned
  and scaled)
100 g (3½ oz) Chinese cabbage,
  including leaves for steaming
  the fish
1 lemongrass stalk, finely sliced
Handful of Thai sweet basil
80 g (2¾ oz) green beans, sliced
  into 2.5-cm (1-in) pieces
80 g (2¾ oz) carrots, peeled and
  chopped into 2.5-cm (1-in)
  slices
50 g (1½ oz) broccoli
50 g (1½ oz) baby corn
50 g (1½ oz) courgettes
Lettuce leaves and cucumber
  slices, to serve

Make the sauce and set aside to cool.

Rinse the fish and pat dry. Arrange some of the Chinese cabbage leaves on a plate, place the lemongrass and sweet basil on to the cabbage and lay the fish on top. (If you are using one whole fish, stuff the lemongrass and sweet basil into the cavity.)

Bring water to the boil in the bottom half of a steamer, place the plate in it, cover and steam for 15–18 minutes. After 10 minutes add the vegetables to be cooked, or steam them separately if it is more convenient. Both the fish and the vegetables must be piping hot when you serve them with the spicy sauce. Add lettuce leaves and cucumber slices to serve.

Hot
Serves 4 as part of a Thai meal
Preparation and cooking time: 1 hour

crying tiger

suer roong hai

This is a very special dish from Isan. Legend has it that it owes its name to a time when the many tigers that roamed the thick forests there would come to the villages in search of food, especially cattle. The first tiger would take the best part of the meat, then the second tiger would discover this and cry loudly because it had missed out. Some people also say that the grilling meat makes a noise like a crying tiger – whichever version you favour, the dish is irresistible.

MARINADE
2 teaspoons soy sauce
1 teaspoon oyster sauce
1 teaspoon chilli powder
1 teaspoon ground white
  pepper
1 teaspoon caster sugar
1 teaspoon finely chopped garlic

300 g (10 oz) beef, such as rump
  or sirloin
Lettuce leaves, cucumber slices,
  slices of chilli, cherry tomatoes,
  coriander and mint leaves,
  to serve
100 ml (3½ fl oz) Isan Chilli
  Sauce (see page 139)

Mix all the marinade ingredients together. Marinate for at least 2 hours in the fridge.

Grill or barbecue the beef until medium-rare, or to your taste, then slice into strips and serve with lettuce, cucumber, slices of chilli, cherry tomatoes, coriander and mint leaves and the chilli sauce on the side.

Hot
Serves 4 as part of a Thai meal
Marinating: 2 hours Preparation and cooking time: 25 minutes

Offering alms to the monks is an integral part of the Thai people's daily life.

prawns with chilli, lime and bitter melon

goong chea num pla

The chilled prawns and bitter melon complement the fiery hot sauce in this Thai favourite. Other varieties of melon won't work in this recipe as they are too sweet, so substitute cucumber slices if bitter melon is not available.

200 g (7 oz) small to
  medium–sized fresh raw
prawns, in the shell
1 bitter melon, sliced

SAUCE
Juice of 4 limes
3½ tablespoons fish sauce
1 teaspoon caster sugar
5 chillies, finely chopped
6 garlic cloves, finely chopped,
  plus 1, sliced, to garnish
2 tablespoons finely chopped
  coriander
Whole coriander leaves, to
  garnish

Shell the prawns, devein and remove the heads, but leave the tails on. Rinse the prawns in cold water, put on a plate, cover with clingfilm and place in the fridge to chill.

To make the sauce, mix the lime juice, fish sauce and sugar in a bowl, then add the chopped chillies, garlic and coriander. Arrange the melon slices on a plate, add the chilled prawns and spoon the sauce over them. Garnish with coriander leaves.

Very hot
Serves 4 as part of a Thai meal
Preparation and cooking time: 30 minutes

Glimpse of a Buddha through the lotus flowers at a shrine.

Northern Thailand

Creamy noodles & green chilli dipping sauces

The north of Thailand is mountainous and very fertile, a beautiful area of teak-forested mountainsides, misty valleys, pagoda-like temples and, of course, Thai elephants. This is a meeting place of many cultures, the site of the first kingdoms of Siam. Influences from Myanmar are strong and nomadic hill tribes inhabit the high mountain areas, identified by their decorative and individual style of dress.

Chiang Mai is the busy cultural and food place where visitors base themselves for mountain treks or adventurous car tours. Driving to Chiang Rai near the Laos border, we passed countless little farms growing fruit and vegetables, with ducks, chickens and pigs scratching about in the yards. Stalls along the way sell coconut-based sweet cakes and, one of my childhood favourites, freshly roasted coconuts – whole coconuts roasted over a fire and cracked open to reveal flesh with a nutty, smoky flavour.

Two of the most famous local dishes are *Gaeng Hanglay* (see pages 92–93), a Burmese curry and *Khao Soi* noodles (see pages 94–95), a delicious, multi-cultural hybrid. Like regional dishes anywhere in the world, there is a basic style for these recipes but individual cooks take pride in their own variation. *Gaeng Hanglay* is a favourite centrepiece for celebrations and important occasions and, rather like a roast chicken or turkey with all the trimmings in the West, there are countless

Early morning in the mountains between Mae Hong Song and Chiang Rai, Northern Thailand.

variations – everyone has their own way of preparing it, adding secret ingredients according to taste.

Ginger, turmeric and galangal are the basic flavourings in *Gaeng Hanglay*, which is traditionally made with pork or chicken, although I have made it with beef for this book. For *Khao Soi*, fresh egg noodles are mixed with a creamy sauce and minced pork or the area's flavoursome chicken. I am a huge fan of Chiang Mai Chicken Salad (see pages 86–87), a shredded chicken salad with a spicy sauce, which is all the more delicious because the local chicken tastes just how I think chicken should.

Chiang Mai is also famous for its pork and for sausage-making. For me the smell of barbecuing freshly made *Sai Ouar* sausages (see pages 100–101), seasoned with turmeric, lemongrass, chilli and black pepper, is totally irresistible. *Nem Sor* (see pages 98–99) is another favourite, a great snack of rice balls flavoured with pork, chilli, mint and lime.

The relatively cool climate and rainfall creates good growing conditions for almost anything from tropical fruits and vegetables to cooler-climate varieties. The region's plentiful vegetables are eaten raw or blanched and served with a series of dipping sauces such as *Nam Prik Noom* (see pages 90–91), a thick, pounded chilli dip made with green chillies and eaten with vegetables and sticky rice. *Nam Prik Ong* (see pages 88–89) is a thick spicy dipping sauce made with pork and eaten with fresh vegetables and sticky rice.

As a visitor to the region you will almost certainly enjoy a *khan tok* meal, sitting on the floor around a low table eating a range of Northern dishes served in small bowls. Northern dishes are generally less fiery than say those of Isan, except for potent dipping sauces such as *Nam Prik Noom*, which you will need to tailor carefully to your taste when making it at home.

Evening prayers at Wat Phra That Doi Suthep, Chiang Mai.

chiang mai chicken salad
yum jin gai

Yum Jin Gai in the Northern country dialect means shredded chicken salad with hot and spicy sauce, and the best are made with tasty, free-range chicken.

300 g (10 oz) skinless, boneless
  chicken breasts
500 ml (18 fl oz) Coconut Milk
  (see page 16)
1 teaspoon ground turmeric
½ teaspoon salt

SAUCE
3 tablespoons fish sauce
1 tablespoon fresh lime juice
1½ teaspoons palm sugar
1½ teaspoons chilli powder, or
  to taste
1 lemongrass stalk, finely sliced
4 shallots, thinly sliced
2 spring onions, finely chopped
15 mint leaves
1 tablespoon coriander leaves
Cucumber slices peeled
  lengthways and whole, dried
  chillies, to serve

Place the chicken breasts in a saucepan, cover with coconut milk and add the turmeric. Bring to the boil, reduce the heat and simmer until the chicken is cooked, about 15 minutes. Remove and set aside to drain and cool, then tear the chicken into small pieces, add salt, mix well and set the chicken aside while you prepare the sauce.

In a bowl mix the fish sauce, lime juice and palm sugar, then add the chicken, chilli powder, lemongrass, sliced shallots, spring onions, mint leaves and coriander. Mix well until the chicken is coated with the sauce and serve with cucumber and dried chillies.

Medium-hot
Serves 4 as part of a Thai meal
Preparation and cooking time: 30 minutes

Dating from 1476, Wat Phra That Lampang Luang is one of Northern Thailand's earliest and most impressive temples.

pork and herb dipping sauce
nam prik ong

This classic, spicy dipping sauce recipe is from the Chiang Mai region and is always included in celebrations and festivals when people traditionally sit on the floor and enjoy a range of dishes eaten with sticky rice.

4 slices galangal, finely chopped
8 dried chillies, deseeded and soaked in warm water
5 garlic cloves, peeled and chopped
1½ shallots, finely chopped
½ teaspoon salt
1 teaspoon shrimp paste
15 cherry tomatoes, halved
2 tablespoons vegetable oil
300 g (10½ oz) pork (or chicken) mince
2 tablespoons water
½ tablespoon Tamarind Juice (see pages 16–17)
½ tablespoon fish sauce
3 teaspoons caster sugar
Fresh vegetables, such as lettuce, cucumber, Thai aubergines, Chinese cabbage leaves, steamed green beans, to serve
2 coriander leaves, to garnish

Using a pestle and mortar, pound the galangal, chillies, garlic, shallots, salt and shrimp paste, then transfer to a mixing bowl. Add the cherry tomatoes and mix together well.

Heat the oil in a wok, add the pounded paste and cook until golden-brown, add the pork and cook for a further 10 minutes. Reduce the heat, add the water, tamarind juice, fish sauce and sugar and simmer for 5 minutes, stirring often, until the dip thickens.

Serve in a bowl with the fresh vegetables arranged on a plate beside it ready for dipping and garnish with coriander.

Medium-hot
Serves 4 as part of a Thai meal
Preparation and cooking time: 30 minutes

Colourful temple offerings at a festival in Chiang Mai.

pounded green chilli dip
nam prik noom

Translated literally, this means "young, unripe chillies made for dipping". Only use green chillies for this – you'll need some small and some large to balance the spicy taste. If you want this very hot use only small chillies; for a milder taste use only large green chillies.

100 g (3½ oz) small green,
   unripe chillies
5 large green chillies
5 shallots, unpeeled
12 garlic cloves, unpeeled
3 medium tomatoes
4 Thai aubergines
2 tablespoons fish sauce
2 tablespoons fresh lime juice
1 teaspoon palm sugar
1 tablespoon finely chopped
   shallot
Slices of chilli

Grill the chillies, whole shallots, garlic, tomatoes and aubergines under a medium heat until the skins brown, about 7 minutes. Leave to cool. When cool enough to handle, peel off the skins.

Halve the tomatoes and aubergines then, using a pestle and mortar, pound the tomatoes, aubergines, chillies, shallots and garlic to a fine paste. Transfer the paste to a bowl and add the fish sauce, lime juice and palm sugar, mixing well until the sugar dissolves.

Sprinkle the dip with chopped shallot and slices of chilli and serve with barbecued meat, Chiang Mai Northern Sausage (see pages 100–101), sticky rice, fresh or steamed vegetables or with pork crackers (see page 16). This dip can be kept in an airtight, sterilized jar in the refrigerator for two or three weeks (see page 14).

Medium-hot
Serves 4 as part of a Thai meal
Preparation and cooking time: 1 hour

Main Buddha at Wat Mahathat, Sukhothai.

northern-style beef curry
gaeng hanglay

Traders and teak loggers from Myanmar introduced this rich and fragrant curry to Chiang Mai, originally using fatty pork without coconut milk to make the dish and eating it with plenty of rice to give them energy. Today *Gaeng Hanglay* is made in many different ways and is a delicacy often served in large quantities for special occasions. Beef simmered in coconut milk gives the curry a rich flavour.

600 ml (1 pt) Coconut Milk
 (see page 16)
Gaeng Hanglay Paste (see
 page 14)
800 g (1 lb 10 oz) beef, such as
 topside, cut into chunks
300 ml (10 fl oz) water
1 tablespoon soy sauce
2 tablespoons fish sauce
2 tablespoons Tamarind Juice
 (see pages 16–17)
2 tablespoons roasted, unsalted
 peanuts
2 tablespoons finely sliced root
 ginger (about 30 g /1 oz)
½ tablespoon palm sugar
Whole, fresh chillies to garnish

Place 300 ml (10 fl oz) of the coconut milk in a flameproof casserole dish and heat over a medium heat until it boils, then add the *Gaeng Hanglay* paste and simmer until the oil separates and rises to the surface, about 8 to 10 minutes. Add the beef, stirring to mix well. Simmer, uncovered, for about 20 minutes then add the remaining coconut milk and the water. Bring back to the boil and simmer until the beef is tender, about 2 hours.

Add the other ingredients, stir well to mix, garnish and serve with rice.

Spicy
Serves 4 as part of a Thai meal
Preparation and cooking time: 3 hours

The Karen (Kariang) hill-tribe people, originally from Myanmar.

chiang mai noodles

khao soi

One of the most popular noodle dishes from the Northern region, originally introduced by the Chinese Haw people, Chiang Mai Noodles combine a rich, creamy sauce with the softness of boiled noodles and the contrasting crunchiness of the crispy-fried ones that are used as a garnish. Use fresh egg noodles for the best results.

200 ml (7 fl oz) vegetable oil, for deep-frying

300 g (10 oz) fresh thin egg noodles

400 ml (13 fl oz) Coconut Milk (see page 16)

1 tablespoon Chiang Mai Noodle paste (see page 15)

120 g (4 oz) skinless, boneless chicken breast, sliced

1 tablespoon medium curry powder

400 ml (14 fl oz) Chicken Stock (see page 138)

2 tablespoons fish sauce

1 tablespoon soy sauce

1½ (2¾ pt) water

1 teaspoon chilli powder

2 spring onions, finely sliced

8 coriander leaves

Crispy-fried chillies

1 lime, quartered

Heat the oil in a deep, heavy-bottomed saucepan and deep-fry 50 g (2 oz) of the noodles until crispy. Remove, drain and set aside to use as garnish.

Heat 200 ml (7 fl oz) of the coconut milk in a saucepan and add the paste, stirring for a minute or so until the paste oil separates and rises to the surface. Add the chicken and simmer for 5 minutes, then add the curry powder, followed by the remaining coconut milk and the chicken stock. Season with the fish sauce and soy sauce and simmer for a further 10 minutes, or until the chicken is cooked.

Reduce the heat to very low to keep the chicken warm. Bring the water to the boil in a separate saucepan and cook the remaining fresh egg noodles for about 1 minute, then stir and drain. Transfer the noodles to individual bowls, pour over the chicken and coconut milk sauce and top with crispy noodles. Sprinkle over a little chilli powder, sliced spring onions, coriander leaves and crispy-fried chillies and serve each portion with a wedge of lime.

Spicy
Serves 4 as part of a Thai meal
Preparation and cooking time: 1 hour

sukhothai noodles

guay teow sukhothai

Unlike many noodle recipes, which are quick to prepare, this one takes a few hours because the soup is made from scratch. Timing the noodles and the final additions to the soup is important if you want to serve this hot – Thailand is a tropical country where food doesn't need to be hot when served but elsewhere there will be a need for a warming bowl of delicious noodles on a cold winter's day. Roasted chilli powder, chopped peanuts, fried garlic and an extra spoonful of sugar are favourite Thai additions.

1 kg (2 lb 4 oz) pork leg bone

3 L (5¼ pt) water

4 garlic cloves, peeled

2 coriander roots

1 teaspoon salt

2 teaspoons dried shrimps

400 g (14 oz) pork fillet

2 teaspoons ground white
  pepper

3 tablespoons fish sauce

1 tablespoon soy sauce

1 tablespoon caster sugar

4 tablespoons vegetable oil

1 tablespoon chopped garlic

1½ L (2¾ pt) water, for
  boiling the noodles

375 g (13 oz) medium rice stick
  noodles, soaked in warm water
  for about 15 minutes

100 g (3½ oz) snake beans (or
  green beans)

150 g (5 oz) beansprouts

2 tablespoons finely chopped
  coriander

2 tablespoons finely chopped
  spring onion

Wash the pork bone, put it in a large stockpot and pour over the water. Bring to the boil then add the whole garlic cloves, coriander roots, salt and dried shrimps. Reduce the heat a little and simmer for 3 hours, skimming every so often to remove the scum that rises to the surface.

Add the pork fillet to the stockpot and cook until it is done, but not breaking up – this takes about 30 minutes. Remove the meat and set aside to cool, then cut into slices about 2.5 cm (1 in) thick. Add the white pepper, fish sauce, soy sauce and sugar to the stock and continue to simmer.

Heat the vegetable oil in a small frying pan and fry the chopped garlic until golden-brown, then remove the pan from the heat immediately to avoid burning the garlic. Set aside the garlic-flavoured oil to add to the noodles when you are ready to serve.

Bring the water for cooking the noodles to the boil in a saucepan, add the noodles and stir to prevent sticking. Cook for about 3 minutes, until just soft (don't overcook them). Remove, drain and divide the noodles equally among four bowls.

Meanwhile, bring the soup back to the boil, add the snake beans and cook for 2 minutes then add the beansprouts and cook for a further 30 seconds. Lift out the beans and beansprouts and place on one side of the noodles. Arrange the pork slices on the other side, add ladlefuls of soup and the garlic oil and stir in the chopped coriander and spring onion. Garnish and serve with Chilli Vinegar (see page 141).

Spicy
Serves 4 as part of a Thai meal
Preparation and cooking time: 4 hours

deep-fried rice balls with chilli and lime

nem sor

Some people claim this is a Vietnamese dish, while others insist it is a Northern Thai dish. Either way, it makes a wonderful snack. *Nem* is a local word for preserved pork (pork, pork skin, garlic, chilli and salt, wrapped in banana leaves to preserve it). Here pork mince is used, to translate the recipe for home cooking. Don't be put off by the pork skin – it gives a more authentic flavour.

200 g (7 oz) cooked rice

2 kaffir lime leaves, finely sliced

1 tablespoon Red Curry Paste
 (see page 15)

50 g (2 oz) shredded coconut

1 teaspoon salt

3 tablespoons plain flour

7 tablespoons water

500 ml (18 fl oz) vegetable oil,
 for deep-frying, plus
 2 tablespoons for cooking the
 pork mince

200 g (7 oz) pork mince

2½ tablespoons fresh lime juice

2 tablespoons fish sauce

1 teaspoon sugar

50 g (2 oz) cooked, Shredded
 Pork Skin (see page 16)

2 tablespoons finely chopped
 spring onion

3 shallots, finely sliced

Handful of mint leaves

16 crispy-fried chillies, lettuce
 and coriander leaves, to garnish

Mix the rice with the lime leaves, red curry paste, shredded coconut and ½ teaspoon of the salt in a bowl and, using your hands, form the mixture into 6 golfball-sized balls. In another bowl, mix the flour and water together to make a batter then roll the balls in it to coat them. Heat the oil for deep-frying in a deep, heavy-bottomed frying pan and deep-fry the rice balls for 3–4 minutes, until golden-brown. Remove, drain and set aside to cool.

Heat 2 tablespoons oil in a wok and cook the pork mince until it is done, about 5 minutes. In a separate bowl combine the lime juice, fish sauce and sugar and mix until the sugar dissolves. Add the cooked pork mince, shredded pork skin, spring onion, shallots and the rice balls, roughly broken up into pieces. Add the mint leaves and mix together, then serve garnished with crispy-fried chillies, lettuce leaves and coriander. Make extra rice balls to serve whole if you wish.

Medium-hot
Makes 6
Preparation and cooking time: 1 hour 30 minutes

Painting on the wall of the Wat Phra That Lampang Luang.

chiang mai northern sausage

sai ouar

This is the traditional lean and tasty pork sausage of Northern Thailand spiced with black pepper, chilli and turmeric. In Chiang Mai you find them being freshly grilled – the smell is irresistible and Thais buy them to eat with the equally irresistible steamed sticky rice.

4 lemongrass stalks, finely chopped

1 tablespoon chilli powder

8 garlic cloves, peeled and finely chopped

4 shallots, peeled and finely chopped

4 coriander roots

500 g (1 lb 2 oz) pork mince with some fat

4 teaspoons sea salt

4 teaspoons caster sugar

8 tablespoons chopped coriander

1 teaspoon freshly ground black pepper

4 teaspoons chopped galangal

1 teaspoon ground turmeric

4 kaffir lime leaves, finely sliced

12 sausage casings (bought from the butcher)

Using a pestle and mortar, pound the lemongrass, chilli powder, garlic, shallots and coriander roots to a fine paste.

In a bowl combine the pork mince with all the remaining ingredients (except the sausage casings) and mix well. Stuff the sausage casings evenly with the mixture to make about 12 sausages.

Prick the sausages with a fork and barbecue, grill or fry. Delicious served with sticky rice, lettuce, chillies, cashew nuts and spring onions.

Spicy
Serves 4 as part of a Thai meal
Preparation and cooking time: 1 hour

Barbecued sausages sizzling in the Chiang Mai markets.

The South
Seafood & spice

My memories of visits to the exotic south of Thailand are of smiling faces, the relaxed atmosphere, the beautiful turquoise colour of the sea and, not surprisingly for an area with two such lengthy coastlines, the sensational fresh seafood.

Platters of shellfish such as huge, juicy prawns, crabs and lobster, large bowls of yellow fish curry made with pungent spices and coconut, bright fruits and vegetables, all served against the backdrop of the sea, are signature images of Southern Thailand. Apart from the visual impact, the tastes are particular to the South – salty from the shrimp paste and fish sauce used in happy abundance, hot with chilli and pungent with spices that were originally introduced here by coastal traders.

Less sweet than the dishes of Central Thailand, curries here are invariably yellow through the addition of turmeric or saffron and some are spiced with cinnamon, cardamom or cloves. All of these signify a Southern dish. *Gaeng Mussaman* (see pages 114–115) is a famous example, a particularly spicy, rich curry which we make with potatoes and beef shank at the Arun Thai to withstand the long cooking time. This dish may take some practice to balance all of the tastes to your liking. *Gaeng Leung Pla* (see pages 112–113) is the local spicy yellow fish curry made with a range of vegetables, and *Khao Mok Gai* (see pages 120–121) is a chicken curry made with cinnamon and cloves as well as turmeric and served with saffron rice.

The recipes I have included here for dishes such as Steamed Mussels with Lemongrass and Sweet Basil (see

Sunset over the Ko Hai rock islands in the Andaman Sea near Trang.

pages 118–119), Chicken Soup with Lime and Turmeric (see pages 106–107) and Hot and Sour Yellow Fish Curry (see pages 112–113) will give you an immediate insight into the Southern style.

Visiting Southern Thailand you might find some of the favourite tastes surprising, such as the prized durian, a fruit which smells terrible but tastes delicious. Signs on hotel doors will warn you that this fruit is not to be brought inside. The large, bitter twisted or stink (sator) beans are another Southern favourite and I have included the recipe for Sator Pad Goong (see pages 116–117), where they are paired with stir-fried prawns, as it is an important part of Southern cuisine. For me memories of the South also include mackerel steamed in a basket and sold cooked in every market. Once plentiful, this is now more of a speciality dish. The same goes for bird's nests, generally believed in Asia to have health-giving and aphrodisiac properties and traditionally collected by gypsies living in thatched huts near the water who collect the empty nests by using ladders to scale the cliffs.

During our visits for research and photography for this book, photographer Ken Martin and I flew from Bangkok to Trang to begin our first journey around the South. We drove through the rubber plantations to Pak Meng on the west coast and pulled up under the casuarina trees at a restaurant beside the beach. The owner brought snacks and beers and, of course, we talked about local food, what was available and, specifically, what we would like to eat that evening. Watching people wade out to net the shellfish fresh for dinner was, for me, the very essence of the Thai experience – Thai people welcoming you to their homes and their restaurants will always serve you the very best of what they have available.

Fishing villages like this one at Pak Meng supply the daily seafood markets.

chicken soup with lime and turmeric

gai tom kha min

This soup isn't so much spicy as rich, from the stock, and earthy from the turmeric. Balanced with lime and fish sauce, this classic dish from Southern Thailand is especially good made with corn-fed or free-range chicken.

2 garlic cloves, peeled

2 shallots, peeled and finely sliced

30 g (1 oz) fresh turmeric root or 1 teaspoon ground turmeric

750 ml (1¼ pt) Chicken Stock (see page 138)

250 ml (8 fl oz) Coconut Milk (see page 16)

4 kaffir lime leaves, torn

200 g (7 oz) skinless, boneless chicken breasts, cut into fine strips

4 tablespoons fish sauce

2½ tablespoons fresh lime juice

1 teaspoon caster sugar

8 baby corn cobs

4 field mushrooms, quartered

8 crispy-fried chillies and coriander leaves, to garnish

Using a pestle and mortar, pound the garlic, sliced shallots and turmeric to a fine paste.

Heat the chicken stock and coconut milk in a medium saucepan then add the paste, kaffir lime leaves and chicken strips and boil together for 8–10 minutes.

Add the fish sauce, lime juice and sugar to the soup then add the baby corn and mushrooms. Simmer for about 2 minutes then serve immediately. Garnish with crispy-fried chillies and coriander leaves.

Spicy
Serves 4 as part of a Thai meal
Preparation and cooking time: 30 minutes

Growers bring their fresh herbs and vegetables to the morning markets every day at Surat Thani on the Gulf of Thailand.

crispy fish with tai pla sauce

gaeng tai pla

Tai Pla is an infamously pungent, salty sauce made from fish innards fermented in barrels with salt for over a year. You don't have to make the sauce – just look for a bottle at your local Asian grocery store.

1 teaspoon shrimp paste

6 garlic cloves, peeled

1 lemongrass stalk, finely chopped

4 small red chillies, chopped

1 teaspoon grated lime rind

1 teaspoon ground turmeric

800 ml (1¼ pt) Fish Stock (see page 138)

3 tablespoons *tai pla* sauce

100 g (3½ oz) bamboo shoots

100 g (3½ oz) green beans

50g (1½ oz) Thai aubergines or twisted beans (*sator*)

3 teaspoons caster sugar

6 kaffir lime leaves, torn

400 g (13½ oz) fish, such as sole or plaice, deep-fried

Put the shrimp paste in a foil parcel and roast for 8 minutes at 160°C (325°F) Gas Mark 3. Using a pestle and mortar pound the garlic, lemongrass, chopped chillies, grated lime rind and turmeric until fine, then mix in the roasted shrimp paste.

Put the fish stock in a medium saucepan and bring to the boil, then add the *tai pla* sauce and the pounded paste. Cook for about 4 minutes then add the bamboo shoots, green beans and Thai aubergines. Add the sugar and torn kaffir lime leaves. Cook until the vegetables are tender but still crisp to the bite, then add the deep-fried fish, stir well and cook briefly, until the fish is heated through.

Very hot
Serves 4 as part of a Thai meal
Preparation and cooking time: 1 hour

Fish drying on nets in the sun at a fishing village in Phuket.

lamb in yellow curry
gaeng khari gae

This is our special recipe, cooked for 17 years in our two restaurants. Originally created by Ell, one of our respected curry chefs who lived in Southern Thailand for a long time, she brings the best traditions of old Southern cuisine to our kitchens. This recipe also works well with meats such as venison or wild boar.

200 ml (7 fl oz) coconut cream

2 tablespoons Red Curry Paste
(see page 15)

800 g (1 lb 12 oz) lean leg of
lamb, boned and cut into
chunks

800 ml (1¼ pt) Coconut Milk
(see page 16)

100 g (3½ oz) onions, roughly
chopped

1 teaspoon ground turmeric

1 tablespoon medium or hot
yellow curry powder with a
high turmeric content

6 tablespoons fish sauce

3 tablespoons palm sugar

12 small potatoes

4 small onions

Coriander leaves, sliced, fresh
chilli and fried shallots to
garnish

Cucumber Relish (see page 141)

Heat the coconut cream in a large saucepan over a low heat, add the red curry paste and cook, stirring until the curry paste oil separates and rises to the surface.

Add the chunks of lamb and mix together well, add the coconut milk and bring to the boil, then add the chopped onion and simmer (uncovered) for 3 hours, until the meat is tender.

Add the turmeric, curry powder, fish sauce, palm sugar, potatoes and small onions and cook until the potatoes are tender. Garnish and serve with the cucumber relish.

Medium-hot
Serves 4 as part of a Thai meal
Preparation and cooking time: About 4 hours

Bargaining for the best price for the day's supplies.

hot and sour yellow fish curry

gaeng leung pla

One of the most popular Southern yellow curries, this dish is extremely hot, spicy and sour. The locals use this method to prepare a wide range of seafood, including the impressively large king prawns that are found in the area and all sorts of vegetables. This is a liquid-style curry to be eaten with plain rice.

1 teaspoon shrimp paste

10 red chillies or to taste, chopped

30 g (1 oz) fresh turmeric root, peeled and finely chopped (or 1 teaspoon ground turmeric)

5 garlic cloves, peeled and chopped

4 shallots, peeled and chopped

1 L (1¾ pt) Fish Stock (see page 138)

600 g (1 lb 5 oz) white fish fillets, cut into chunks

200 g (7 oz) Chinese cabbage leaves

150 g (5 oz) sliced bamboo shoots

150 g (5 oz) broccoli or cauliflower florets

7 tablespoons fish sauce

4 tablespoons fresh lime juice

4 tablespoons Tamarind Juice (see pages 16–17)

Wrap the shrimp paste in a foil parcel and roast at 160°C (325°F) Gas Mark 3 for about 5–7 minutes, until it is dry. Take care not to burn it.

Using a pestle and mortar, pound the chillies, turmeric, garlic and shallots until fine. Add the roasted shrimp paste and mix together.

Heat the fish stock in a large saucepan, add the pounded ingredients and boil for 5 minutes then add the fish and cook for about 7 minutes, until the fish is cooked through. Add the cabbage, bamboo shoots and broccoli or cauliflower florets and cook until they are tender, about 7 minutes, then season with fish sauce, lime juice and tamarind juice. Serve hot.

Very hot
Serves 4 as part of a Thai meal
Preparation and cooking time: 40 minutes

Longtail speedboats waiting to take tourists to the rock islands at Phi Phi.

mussaman beef curry

gaeng mussaman

This is a spicy Southern Thai curry with Islamic origins. Portuguese traders brought spices such as turmeric, cinnamon, cumin, cloves and nutmeg from the Middle East and India to the south coast of Thailand and the Gulf of Siam at the same time as chilli, and this recipe combines these dry spices with Thai sweet, sour and salty tastes. I use shin or topside of beef because the curry needs to be boiled for up to four hours.

1½ L (2¾ pt) Coconut Milk
  (see page 16)
100 g (3½ oz) Mussaman Curry
  Paste (see page 16)
1 kg (2 lb 4 oz) beef, topside,
  shin or shank, cut into 2.5-cm
  (1-in) pieces
Handful of dried bay leaves (or
  6–7 fresh bay leaves)
12 small potatoes suitable for
  stewing, peeled (or larger
  potatoes, peeled and
  quartered)
8 pickling onions, peeled
5½ tablespoons fish sauce
3 tablespoons palm sugar
7 tablespoons Tamarind Juice
  (see pages 16–17)
Fried onions, coriander leaves
  and slices of chilli, to garnish

Heat 200 ml (7 fl oz) of the coconut milk in a large saucepan and add the mussaman paste, stirring together until the oil from the paste separates and rises to the surface.

Add the beef, stirring well to combine with the coconut milk mixture then add the bay leaves and the remaining coconut milk and simmer for 3 hours, until the beef is tender.

Add the potatoes and onions and simmer for a further hour, until the potatoes are cooked. Season the curry with fish sauce, palm sugar and tamarind juice. Garnish with some fried onions, coriander leaves and slices of chilli.

Spicy
Serves 4 as part of a Thai meal
Preparation and cooking time: 4 hours

Exotic, tropical fruits like mangosteen, green mango and rambutan are delicious served after a spicy Thai curry.

stir-fried prawns with sator beans

goong pad sator

Thai people in the Southern region love the taste of their pungent *sator* – large, flat beans with a strong smell and a bitter taste. Frozen *sator* beans are exported around the world to keep homesick Thais happy, as they find the flavour delicious. These beans are something of an acquired taste, like strong blue cheese – you either love them, smell included, or loathe them.

3 cloves garlic, peeled

3 small red chillies

1 teaspoon shrimp paste

1 tablespoon vegetable oil

8 raw king prawns, shelled and
  deveined

100 g (3½ oz) twisted or
  stink beans (*sator*)

1 tablespoon Chicken Stock (see
  page 138)

2 long red chillies, sliced

1½ tablespoons fish sauce

1 tablespoon oyster sauce

1 teaspoon caster sugar

3 kaffir lime leaves

Using a pestle and mortar, pound the garlic, chillies and shrimp paste together to form a fine paste.

Heat the oil in a wok, add the paste and cook briefly until it releases its aroma. Add the prawns and cook for 3 minutes. Add the beans, stock and sliced chillies and mix well. Cook for a further 2–3 minutes.

Season with fish sauce, oyster sauce and sugar and cook for a further 2 minutes. Add the kaffir lime leaves and serve with plain rice.

Hot
Serves 4 as part of a Thai meal
Preparation and cooking time: 20 minutes

Twisted (sator) beans are shelled and added to stir-fries and curries and can also be eaten raw with dipping sauce.

steamed mussels with lemongrass and sweet basil

hoi maleang phu neung Ta-khrai

Mussels in Thailand are small and tasty. The little ones are best for this recipe, where they are steamed and served with a pungent seafood sauce.

800 g (1 lb 12 oz) fresh mussels,
  in the shell
3 garlic cloves, peeled
3 small red chillies
1 lemongrass stalk, sliced
1 kaffir lime leaf, torn
150 ml (5 fl oz) Fish Stock (see
  page 138)
½ teaspoon salt
Handful of Thai sweet basil
  leaves
Seafood Sauce (see page 140)

Put the mussels in a large pot of cold water and use a brush to scrub and beard them, removing the hairy growth from the shell. Drain and rinse the mussels in clean water. Discard any that fail to close when tapped sharply.

Use a mortar and pestle to pound the garlic and chillies together to form a fine paste. Transfer the paste to a large pan and add the mussels, lemongrass, kaffir lime leaf, fish stock and salt. Steam for about 6 minutes, until the mussels open (discard any that fail to open), transfer to a bowl, garnish with basil leaves, and serve with the seafood sauce.

Medium-hot
Serves 4 as part of a Thai meal
Preparation and cooking time: 25 minutes

Buddhas covered in gleaming gold-leaf.

saffron rice with chicken
khao mok gai

Dishes featuring saffron rice originate from Southern Thailand. *Khao Mok Gai* is often cooked in a big pot and served at special family occasions such as weddings and other religious ceremonies. Guests traditionally sit on the floor and eat this dish as part of a feast which usually includes a fish or meat curry. If you prefer, substitute ground turmeric for the saffron.

500 ml (18 fl oz) vegetable oil,
  for deep-frying, plus extra for
  stir-frying
500 g (1 lb 2 oz) jasmine rice
½ teaspoon saffron strands (or
  1 teaspoon ground turmeric)
750 ml (24 fl oz) Chicken Stock
  (see page 138) or water
2 teaspoons salt
½ teaspoon ground white
  pepper
8 chicken drumsticks
4 cardamom pods
4 fresh bay leaves, torn
2 shallots, peeled, finely sliced
  and fried
Slices of chilli and coriander
  leaves, to garnish
Cucumber Relish (see page 141)

Heat a little oil in a wok and stir-fry the rice with the saffron to mix together, then add the stock. Season with the salt and pepper, cover and cook for 10 minutes.

Heat the oil and deep-fry the chicken drumsticks until the skin is golden-brown, about 5 minutes. Remove the drumsticks, draining carefully, and add to the cooking rice together with the cardamom pods and the torn bay leaves. Boil to reduce the stock, then reduce the heat and simmer for about 20 minutes until the rice is cooked and all the liquid has been absorbed.

Sprinkle the fried shallots, sliced chilli and coriander leaves over the chicken and rice and serve with cucumber relish.

Mild
Serves 4 as part of a Thai meal
Preparation and cooking time: 35 minutes

Tasty native chickens barbecuing Thai-style over charcoal.

Thai "Tapas"
Khap klaem

Snacks and appetizers to go with drinks are called *khap klaem*, literally "drinking food", like Spanish tapas – a surprising custom in a largely Buddhist country, but very much a part of Thai life, like going to a bar after work in any city.

From the age of five I lived with my grandfather, grandmother and two aunties in a two-storey house in Isan in Northeastern Thailand. They owned a general store selling everything from clothes to fishing tackle. We had a fridge in one corner, the only one in the area, so had precious ice for cold drinks and sold beer and whisky. There were a few tables outside and customers would sit and drink and we prepared snacks for them.

We served betel leaf (*meang khum*) spicy nuts with coriander and chilli, deep-fried snacks (*yum*), Thai salads and grilled or barbecued meat or fish including satays and Isan sausages. Today this tradition continues and both working men and women stay in town after work to have a drink at bars or corner stores and eat snacks, before moving on to a restaurant to catch up with friends and family for dinner.

Now we have created our own Thai "tapas" bar here at the Arun Thai restaurant with a menu of dishes changing weekly. Recipes for some of the dishes follow in this chapter and others are scattered throughout the book, such as Crying Tiger beef (see pages 78–79), Stir-Fried Clams with Chilli and Basil (see pages 46–47), Isan Duck Salad (see pages 64–65), Prawns with Chilli, Lime and Bitter Melon (see pages 80–81) and Chiang Mai Northern Sausage (see pages 100–101).

Thai "tapas" (khap klaem) are served at the Crying Tiger Bar at the Arun Thai restaurant, Sydney.

prawns in pastry
goong hom sabai

The name literally means "prawns with a sash", representing the sash traditionally worn by Thai women on formal occasions. The pastry wrapping takes a bit of practice; don't forget to leave the prawn tail outside the pastry when you begin to roll it up.

8 uncooked king prawns,
  shelled
1 tablespoon soy sauce
1 teaspoon caster sugar
¼ teaspoon ground white
  pepper
6 spring roll sheets
  (25 x 25cm/10 x 10 in)
1 egg yolk, beaten
500 ml (18 fl oz) vegetable oil

PASTE
6 uncooked prawns
¼ teaspoon ground white
  pepper
½ teaspoon caster sugar
½ tablespoon soy sauce

Using a sharp knife, score the king prawns diagonally towards the tail on both sides and horizontally underneath. This will prevent them from curling up as they cook. Mix the soy sauce, caster sugar and white pepper in a bowl and add the prawns to marinate.

Using a blender, mix the paste ingredients together until very fine and set aside.

Cut the spring roll sheets in half diagonally, cutting a slice off one corner and placing that at the centre of the sheet. Spread one teaspoon of paste over the pastry piece in the centre (this forms an extra layer to prevent moisture seeping through the pastry) then lay a king prawn on the sheet with the tail outside and roll up tightly, enfolding the prawn. Seal the edges with beaten egg yolk. Repeat with all the prawns. Heat the vegetable oil and deep-fry the rolls for 10 minutes. Drain on kitchen paper. Serve plain or on a bed of crispy-fried noodles and chopped chilli as shown.

Mild
Makes 8
Preparation and cooking time: 35 minutes

Buddha at Wat Phra That Doi Suthep, Chiang Mai.

fresh oysters with spicy thai sauce

hoi nang rom sood

Oysters are farmed in the Central and Southern regions of Thailand. The best-known, from the Surat Thani area, are large and succulent. Use only the freshest oysters for this recipe.

2 garlic cloves, peeled and very
    finely sliced
1 small red chilli, finely sliced
1 shallot, peeled, sliced and
    crispy-fried
3 tablespoons fresh lime juice
2 tablespoons Chilli Sauce (see
    page 139)
24 freshly shucked oysters
Crushed ice
Finely sliced carrot and
    coriander leaves, to garnish

Place the garlic/chilli, shallot, lime juice and chilli sauce into individual little serving dishes.

Arrange the oysters on crushed ice on individual dishes or a large platter and serve them immediately as they should be chilled. Garnish with sliced carrot and coriander leaves. Add a small amount of each ingredient to each oyster in its shell before eating.

Spicy
Serves 4 as part of a Thai meal
Preparation and cooking time: 30 minutes

Wild orchids grow profusely in Northern Thailand.

betel leaves
meang khum

Wrapping these tasty ingredients in crunchy betel nut leaves is a tradition at the Arun Thai – the leaves are seasonal, so customers are always asking when they will be available. In Thailand Chinese broccoli leaves can also be used as they share a similar nutty, "grassy" taste which complements the bright flavours of the other ingredients.

SAUCE

1 teaspoon shrimp paste

1 teaspoon vegetable oil

1 teaspoon finely chopped
   galangal (optional)

1 teaspoon finely chopped
   shallot

1 tablespoon finely chopped
   root ginger

1 teaspoon dried shrimps, finely
   blended

4 tablespoons toasted, shredded
   coconut

5 tablespoons water

3 tablespoons palm sugar

1 tablespoon fish sauce

12 betel nut leaves (or Chinese
   broccoli leaves)

2 tablespoons roasted, unsalted
   peanuts

2 tablespoons dried shrimps

2 tablespoons diced root ginger

2 tablespoons diced lime (skin on)

2 tablespoons diced shallot

80 g (2¾ oz) toasted, shredded
   coconut

2 chillies sliced into rings

First make the sauce. Wrap the shrimp paste in foil and grill it for 2–3 minutes, until the paste is dry. Heat the oil in a small pan then add the galangal, shallot and ginger and stir for 2 minutes to aromatize. Add the dried shrimps, shredded coconut, water, shrimp paste, palm sugar and fish sauce and stir over a low heat until the sauce thickens. The consistency should be quite sticky and the taste both salty and sweet. Remove the sauce from the heat and set aside to cool.

Arrange all the ingredients separately on a serving platter. To serve, spoon on a little of each ingredient on to a betel nut leaf (except the toasted coconut and fresh chilli which are to taste) and top with a teaspoon of the sauce. Wrap the leaf into a bite-sized piece and enjoy!

Medium-hot – hot
Serves 4 as part of a Thai meal
Preparation and cooking time: 1 hour

The afternoon markets in Nakhon Pathom sell snacks and selections of ready-cooked food to eat on-the-spot or take home.

chicken in pandanus leaves
gai hor bai toey

Marinated chicken wrapped in aromatic pandanus leaves makes a wonderful snack or starter. This is the only meat dish made with pandanus leaves in Thailand as they are usually used for flavouring desserts and sticky rice. The leaves infuse the chicken with their earthy, vanilla aroma and are tied tightly to keep out the oil. The parcels must be unwrapped as the pandanus leaf is not eaten. Fresh or frozen pandanus leaves can be found in specialist Asian food shops.

5 garlic cloves, peeled and finely
   chopped
4 coriander roots
1 teaspoon ground white
   pepper
1 tablespoon caster sugar
3 tablespoons oyster sauce
2 tablespoons light soy sauce
500 g (1 lb 2 oz) chicken thigh
   fillets, trimmed of fat, each
   cut into four
12–14 pandanus leaves
500 ml (18 fl oz) vegetable oil
   for frying
Finely sliced carrot, to garnish

SAUCE
5 tablespoons dark soy sauce
4 tablespoons palm sugar
1 teaspoon white sesame seeds,
   toasted

Using a pestle and mortar, pound the garlic and coriander until fine then transfer to a bowl.

Add the pepper, sugar, oyster sauce and soy sauce to the bowl. Mix well, making sure the sugar has dissolved, add the chicken, cover and place in the fridge to marinate overnight.

When you are ready to cook, you can wrap the chicken in the pandanus leaves in two ways:

1. Make a triangle with the pandanus leaf, placing the chicken in the centre then wrapping tightly and securing with a cocktail stick.
2. Take a pandanus leaf and twist the left end into the middle of the leaf to create a hollow. Place two of the chicken cubes (4 x 4 cm/1½ x 1½ in) in the hollow, then feed the right end through the hole and tighten both ends as if tying a bow. Tie tightly so the cooking oil can't seep into the filling and cut both ends, leaving about 2.5 cm (1 in) at each end.

Make the sauce by simmering the soy sauce and sugar together in a small saucepan, stirring until the palm sugar has dissolved. Transfer to a small bowl for serving, and top with the toasted sesame seeds.

Heat the oil in a heavy-bottomed frying pan to 160°C (325°F) and deep-fry the chicken in pandanus leaves for 3–5 minutes. Unwrap the parcels and discard the leaves. Check that the chicken is cooked. Serve the chicken with the sauce. Garnish with sliced carrot.

Mild
Serves 4 as part of a Thai meal
Marinate: Overnight Preparation and cooking time: 30 minutes

chicken satay

gai satay

Satays are a Malaysian-Indonesian dish from Southern Thailand. Our chicken version is sweet and aromatic from the turmeric and garlic, rather than hot or spicy. This is served with its own satay sauce made with peanuts, coconut milk and palm sugar. The satays can also be served with Cucumber Relish (see page 141).

1 tablespoon yellow curry
  powder
1 tablespoon chopped garlic
½ teaspoon ground white
  pepper
1 teaspoon ground turmeric
1 teaspoon salt
5 tablespoons caster sugar
4 tablespoons fish sauce
500 g (1 lb 2 oz) skinless,
  boneless chicken breasts, sliced
  into strips 6-cm (2½-in) long
  and 1½-cm (⅝-in) wide
Coconut Milk (see page 16),
  for brushing
Cucumber strips, sliced raw
  onion and chilli, to garnish
Satay Sauce, to serve (see page
  140)

Mix the curry powder, garlic, white pepper, turmeric, salt, sugar and fish sauce together, add the chicken, cover and place in the fridge to marinate overnight.

When you are ready to cook, soak wooden skewers in water for 15 minutes to prevent the ends from burning during cooking. Thread the marinated chicken pieces on to the pre-soaked wooden skewers, brush with coconut milk and barbecue or grill for about 3 minutes, until cooked. Garnish and serve with satay sauce.

Mild
Serves 4 as part of a Thai meal
Marinate: overnight Preparation and cooking time: 30 minutes

Street vendors grill their satays on the pavements of Bangkok.

fresh spring rolls

popai sood

Spring rolls are usually served crispy-fried but these freshly wrapped rolls are an alternative, full of tasty crab, beansprouts, garlic, cucumber and tofu. Served with a warm sauce they make tasty snacks or starters.

OMELETTE
3 eggs
Pinch of salt
2 teaspoons vegetable oil

SAUCE
1 tablespoon vegetable oil
1 clove garlic, peeled and finely
  chopped
2 teaspoons palm sugar
150 ml (5 fl oz) water
4 tablespoons Tamarind Juice
  (see pages 16–17)
1 long red chilli, finely chopped
1 teaspoon salt
2 teaspoons cornflour dissolved
  in 2 tablespoons water

150 ml (5 fl oz) water
2 garlic cloves, peeled and
  crushed
½ teaspoon salt
100 g (3½ oz) white crabmeat
60 g (2 oz) firm tofu (beancurd),
  cut into 7½ x 1-cm (3 x ½-in)
  pieces
60 g (2 oz) cooked beansprouts
3 (25 x 25-cm/10 x 10-in) spring
  roll sheets
1 cucumber, cut into 7½ x 1-cm
  (3 x ½-in) strips
Slices of chilli and coriander
  leaves, to garnish

First make the omelette. Beat the eggs in a bowl and add the salt. Heat the oil in a frying pan. Add half the egg mixture and cook until dry on one side, then turn and continue to cook until you have a very thin omelette. Remove from the pan. Cook the remaining mixture in the same way. When the omelettes are cool, slice into thin strips.

Now make the sauce. Heat the oil in a saucepan, add the garlic and stir until golden-brown then add the sugar, water, tamarind juice, chopped chilli and salt. Stir continuously until the mixture boils. Add the cornflour and water mixture and mix well, stirring until the sauce thickens. Reduce the heat to keep the sauce just warm while you prepare the spring rolls.

Bring the water to the boil in a saucepan and add the garlic, salt and crabmeat. Cook for 3 minutes. Remove the crabmeat and set aside to drain, then add the tofu to the liquid and cook for 2 minutes. Remove the tofu and set aside to drain while you cook the beansprouts in the liquid for 1 minute. Remove and drain.

Remove one spring roll sheet from the bag (they must remain moist), lay it on a flat surface and spread a third of the omelette slices on top. Add some beansprouts, tofu, cucumber and crabmeat and roll up tightly. Cut into four pieces then repeat with the remaining spring roll sheets. (Reserve a few strips of omelette for garnish.)

Serve immediately, topped with the warm sauce, garnished with slices of chilli, coriander leaves and thin strips of omelette.

Mild
Serves 4 as part of a Thai meal
Preparation and cooking time: 40 minutes

drunken noodles
pad kee mao

This noodle dish is a favourite in Thai bars, pubs and street stalls and is just the thing to enjoy with a drink, or after a drink to sober you up before you go home! Chicken or seafood can be used but this recipe is made with beef.

10 small red chillies

3 garlic cloves, peeled

4 tablespoons vegetable oil

250 g (8 oz) flat noodles (or thin rice stick noodles)

1 tablespoon dark soy sauce

250g (8 oz) finely sliced beef or mince

Handful of holy basil

180 g (6 oz) Chinese broccoli leaves, torn

2 tablespoons sliced onion

2 tablespoons sliced spring onion

1 tablespoon light soy sauce

2 tablespoons fish sauce

1 teaspoon caster sugar

2 tablespoons green peppercorns

Sliced fresh chilli, to serve

Pound the chillies and garlic together using a mortar and pestle. Set aside.

Heat 2 tablespoons of the oil in a wok, add the noodles, stir quickly, then add the dark soy sauce and stir well. Remove from the wok and set aside.

Heat the remaining oil in the wok, add the pounded garlic and chilli paste and cook until brown, then add the beef and cook, stirring until the beef is cooked through. Now add the basil leaves, broccoli leaves, onion, spring onion, light soy sauce, fish sauce, sugar and peppercorns. Mix well, then add the noodles, stirring to combine with the sauce, and serve.

Very hot
Serves 4 as part of a Thai meal
Preparation and cooking time: 45 minutes

Clay mortars and wooden pestles are essential Thai utensils.

stocks, sauces & relishes

Sauces are added to cooked meat and fish, while thicker dipping sauces are actually a dish in their own right made to accompany steamed vegetables, rice or meat. Thais cook their stocks daily to go with dishes including noodles, stir-fries, meat, vegetables and seafood, which is another reason why everything tastes so incredibly fresh.

Chicken stock

Makes 1 L (1¾ pt)
1.5 kg (3 lb) chicken bones
2 L (3½ pt) water
Pinch of salt

Place the bones in the water in a stockpot over a high heat and boil for 20 minutes. Skim off the layer of fat which forms, then lower the heat and simmer the stock until the liquid has reduced to almost half. Add the salt, then remove from the heat and allow to cool. Strain and discard the bones. This stock will keep in the fridge in a sealed container for two weeks.

Fish stock

Makes 1 L (1¾ pt)
2 kg (4½ lb) fish heads and bones from fish such as
   snapper, cod, haddock
2 L (3½ pt) water
Pinch of salt

Heat a wok, add the fish heads and bones and fry for 5 minutes, stirring to prevent burning. Then remove and rinse the bones in boiling water to remove the smell, throwing the water away. In a stockpot, boil the water and add the fish bones. Boil for 5 minutes then simmer until the stock has reduced by about half. Remove from the heat and cool. Strain and discard the bones. This stock keeps for two weeks in a sealed container in the fridge.

Vegetable stock

Makes 1 L (1¾ pt)
150 g (5 oz) Chinese cabbage, cut into pieces
100 g (3½ oz) carrots, peeled and chopped
100g (3½ oz) white radish, chopped
2 L (3½ pt) water
Pinch of salt

Place the vegetables in the water in a stockpot and bring to the boil, then lower the heat and simmer for about an hour until the stock has reduced by about half. Strain and discard the vegetables. This stock will keep for two weeks in a sealed container in the fridge.

Steamed vegetable and fish dipping sauce

pla nung jeew
A typical Isan dipping sauce to serve with many kinds of fresh fish and steamed vegetables.

Makes 100ml (3¼ fl oz)
1 large red chilli
2 small red chillies
3 garlic cloves, unpeeled
2 shallots, unpeeled
3 cherry tomatoes
1½ tablespoons fish sauce
1 tablespoon fresh lime juice

Grill the chillies, garlic, shallots and cherry tomatoes for 10 minutes, until brown. Leave to cool. When cool enough to handle, peel off the skins and, using a pestle and mortar, pound them to a fine paste. Add the fish sauce and lime juice, mix well and set aside to cool – the sauce is served cool as re-heating it makes the lime taste bitter.

Chilli sauce
sriracha sauce

This famous sauce from Sriracha is loved in Asia for its unique flavour which goes perfectly with things like omelettes, pan-fried oysters, seafood and meatballs.

Makes 100 ml (3¼ fl oz)
10 red chillies
10 cloves garlic, peeled
1 tablespoon white vinegar
1 teaspoon salt
1 teaspoon caster sugar
½ tablespoon water

Blend all the ingredients together in a blender for about 5 minutes until fine. Store in an airtight jar in the fridge.

Isan chilli sauce
nam jim jeew

One of the most popular sauces of the Isan region, this goes with dishes such as Crying Tiger (see pages 78–79) and barbecued pork, chicken or fish.

Makes 100 ml (3¼ fl oz)
2 teaspoons chilli powder
2 teaspoons ground roasted rice
½ teaspoon caster sugar
2 tablespoons fresh lime juice
1 tablespoon fish sauce
2 tablespoons light soy sauce
1 teaspoon chopped shallots
1 teaspoon chopped coriander

Mix the chilli paste, ground roasted rice, sugar, lime juice, fish sauce and light soy sauce in a bowl until the sugar has dissolved. Sprinkle on the shallots and coriander and serve.

Breakfast delivery in Chiang Mai – rice is mashed and grilled to make rice wafers.

Satay sauce

nam jim satay

This crunchy sweet sauce is especially made to go with satays and steamed vegetables or salad.

Makes 400 ml (14 fl oz)
400 ml (14 fl oz) Coconut Milk (see page 16)
½ tablespoon Red Curry Paste (see page 15)
125 g (4 oz) roasted peanuts, coarsely ground
5 tablespoons caster sugar
1 teaspoon salt

Heat the coconut milk in a saucepan and add the curry paste, stirring until the oil separates and rises to the surface. Add the ground peanuts and stir until the paste thickens, then add the sugar and salt and serve.

Seafood sauce

nam jim thalay

Delicious with all seafood including dishes of mussels, barbecued prawns and fresh mudcrabs.

Makes 100 ml (3¼ fl oz)
4 garlic cloves, peeled
4 small red chillies
2 coriander roots
Small pinch of sea salt
1 teaspoon sugar
3 tablespoons fresh lime juice
2 tablespoons fish sauce
1 tablespoon chopped coriander

Using a pestle and mortar, pound the garlic, chillies, coriander roots and sea salt together.

Combine the sugar, lime juice and fish sauce in a bowl, stirring until the sugar dissolves. Add the pounded paste and mix well, then sprinkle in the chopped coriander.

Chicken sauce

This is the sauce to serve with barbecued and deep-fried chicken and with starters such as fishcakes.

Makes 100 ml (3¼ fl oz)
3 tablespoons water
100 g (3½ oz) caster sugar
3 tablespoons white wine vinegar
1 long red chilli, chopped
2 pickled garlic cloves, chopped
1 teaspoon salt
1 tablespoon fish sauce

Boil the water with the sugar in a small saucepan, stirring until the sugar dissolves, then add the vinegar. Remove from the heat.

Blend the chilli and pickled garlic until fine and add to the ingredients in the pan. Stir together over a low heat until the sauce thickens. Add the salt and fish sauce and serve.

Fish sauce with chilli

prik nam pla

Every Thai household has their own way of making this flavoursome chilli sauce. It's a real favourite which we love to add to rice.

Makes 40 ml (1⅓ fl oz)
2 chillies, chopped
1½ tablespoons fish sauce
1 teaspoon fresh lime juice

Simply combine the ingredients in a bowl and stir.

Cucumber relish

arjar

This is a delicious accompaniment for all strong curries, including mussaman, venison and lamb and it also goes well with chicken satays. You can keep this relish in an airtight, sterlized jar (see page 14) in the fridge for a couple of months, adding the freshly chopped ingredients to serve.

Makes 450 ml (¾ pt)
225 ml (8 fl oz) water
100 g (3½ oz) caster sugar
125 ml (4 fl oz) white wine vinegar
Pinch of salt
1 cucumber, sliced then the slices quartered
1 shallot, finely sliced
2 small red chillies, finely chopped
4 coriander leaves, to garnish

Boil the water in a small saucepan and add the sugar, stirring until it dissolves. Add the vinegar and salt and remove from the heat. Allow the mixture to cool.

Serve the relish in a small dish or bowl, adding the slices of cucumber, shallot and chillies. Garnish with the coriander leaves.

Chilli vinegar

nam som prik dong

Usually served with Thai noodles in both soups and stir-fried noodle dishes. The chilli can be chopped or left whole, and you can make a larger quantity to store in a jar ready for use.

Makes 35 ml (1⅕ fl oz)
2 chillies, chopped
2 tablespoons vinegar

Combine the chilli and vinegar.

Making crispy-fried prawn cakes with curry powder and curry leaves.

Index

banana flower salad 28

banana leaves, steamed chicken in 75

beef: crying tiger 78
  drunken noodles 136
  Mussaman beef curry 115
  northern-style beef curry 92
  Panang beef 38
  waterfall beef salad 68

betel leaves 128

bitter melon, prawns with chilli, lime and 80

catfish: crispy fish salad with green mango 56

Chiang Mai chicken salad 86

Chiang Mai noodle paste 15

Chiang Mai noodles 94

Chiang Mai northern sausage 100

chicken: banana flower salad 28
  Chiang Mai chicken salad 86
  Chiang Mai noodles 94
  chicken and coconut soup 26
  chicken in pandanus leaves 130
  chicken satay 133
  chicken sauce 140
  chicken soup with lime and turmeric 106
  green chicken curry 32
  jungle chicken curry 30
  papaya salad with barbecued chicken 66
  saffron rice with chicken 120

steamed chicken in banana leaves 75

stock 138

chillies: chilli sauces 139
  chilli vinegar 141
  fish sauce with chilli 140
  pounded green chilli dip 91
  roasted chilli paste 14

clams, stir-fried with chilli and basil 46

coconut, steamed salmon in 41

coconut milk 16
  chicken and coconut soup 26

cooking techniques 16–17

crab: fresh spring rolls 134
  stir-fried crab with yellow curry sauce 51

crying tiger 78

cucumber relish 141

curries: green chicken curry 32
  hot and sour yellow fish curry 112
  jungle chicken curry 30
  lamb in yellow curry 110
  Mussaman beef curry 115
  northern-style beef curry 92
  pan-fried salmon with chu chee curry sauce 44
  Panang beef 38
  red duck curry with pineapple 34
  stir-fried crab with yellow curry sauce 51
  vegetable curry with venison 72

curry pastes 14–16

drunken noodles 136

duck: Isan duck salad 64
  red duck curry with pineapple 34

fish: crispy fish salad with green mango 56
  crispy fish with tai pla sauce 108
  hot and sour fish soup 22
  hot and sour yellow fish curry 112
  Isan sour fish soup 62
  pan-fried salmon with chu chee curry sauce 44
  steamed fish with lime juice and chilli 42
  steamed fish with vegetables and spicy sauce 76
  steamed salmon in young coconut 41
  stock 138

fish sauce with chilli 140

Gaeng Hanglay paste 14

green curry paste 15

ingredients 10–13

Isan duck salad 64

Isan mushroom salad 71

Isan sour fish soup 62

lamb: lamb in yellow curry 110
  stir-fried lamb with holy basil 37

mango, crispy fish salad with 56

mushroom salad, Isan 71

Mussaman beef curry 115

Mussaman curry paste 16

mussels, steamed with lemongrass and sweet basil 118

noodles: Chiang Mai noodles 94
  drunken noodles 136
  stir-fried rice noodles with king prawns 52
  Sukhothai noodles 97

oysters with spicy Thai sauce 126

Panang beef 38

Panang curry paste 15

pandanus leaves, chicken in 130

papaya salad with barbecued chicken 66

peanuts: satay sauce 140
  pineapple, red duck curry with 34

pork: Chiang Mai northern sausage 100
  deep-fried rice balls with chilli and lime 98
  pork and herb dipping sauce 88
  pork crackers 16
  shredded pork skin 16
  Sukhothai noodles 97

prawns: banana flower salad 28
  king prawn soup 25
  prawns in pastry 124
  prawns with chilli, lime and bitter melon 80
  stir-fried prawns with

sator beans 116
stir-fried rice noodles with
king prawns 52
preparation techniques 17

red curry paste 15
rice 16
deep-fried rice balls with
chilli and lime 98
saffron rice with chicken
120

saffron rice with chicken
120
salads: banana flower salad
28
Chiang Mai chicken salad
86

crispy fish salad with
green mango 56
Isan duck salad 64
Isan mushroom salad 71
papaya salad with
barbecued chicken 66
waterfall beef salad 68
salmon: pan-fried salmon
with chu chee curry
sauce 44
steamed salmon in young
coconut 41
satay: chicken satay 133
satay sauce 140
sator beans, stir-fried
prawns with 116
sauces 138–40
sausages, Chiang Mai 100

scampi, stir-fried with
krachai and peppercorns
48
seafood sauce 140
soups: chicken and coconut
soup 26
chicken soup with lime
and turmeric 106
hot and sour fish soup 22
Isan sour fish soup 62
king prawn soup 25
spring rolls: fresh spring
rolls 134
prawns in pastry 124
stocks 138
Sukhothai noodles 97

tamarind juice 16–17

tofu, roasted with chilli,
coriander and
mushrooms 54

vegetables: steamed fish
with spicy sauce and 76
steamed vegetable and
fish dipping sauce
138–9
stock, 138
vegetable curry with
venison 72
venison, vegetable curry
with 72
vinegar, chilli 141

waterfall beef salad 68

About Khamtane Signavong

Kham was born on 13 October, 1962 at Savannakhet on the Lao side of the Mekong River. The name Khamtane, meaning "solid gold" in the Isan language, was given to Kham by a head monk in the city of Mukdahan and Kham, as he is known to his friends and customers of the Arun Thai Restaurant, lived with his grandparents from the age of 4, because his parents were building their business during that time.

"My grandfather came from the central part of Thailand, and he's a very good cook too. The family always looked forward to his cooking and my grandmother took me to the markets which gave me the knowledge of how to select fresh produce such as the best fish, river prawns, crab, frog and eel, as well as the best vegetables, herbs and spices of the day."

"At the age of five I was already eating spicy food and I learnt that from my grandparents, uncle and auntie who are all big chilli eaters. Then, in 1977, my father asked me if I would like to continue my high school studies in Australia and stay with my uncle in Sydney. I was thrilled at the opportunity and, as my uncle and auntie here were busy with their jobs, I helped by cooking and taking care of my two little cousins. That's how I started to cook the traditional Thai cuisine I learned from my grandparents."

In 1987 a cousin of Kham's came to Australia from Thailand and said she'd like to open a Thai restaurant with him. It took them almost one and half years to organize it,

but the Arun Thai Restaurant finally opened in 1988 in Elizabeth Bay and quickly became a favourite.

The name Arun comes from the Wat Arun temple beside the Chao Phraya River in Bangkok. Arun means "dawn" in Thai. In 1995 a second restaurant opened on Sydney's Macleay Street, set up in the 18th-century "Noble House" style and serving the more refined Thai Royal Cuisine style food.

Inspired by friends, Kham also began to build a cellar of wines to complement the food. He has developed an amazing palate and an enviable cellar put together from many years of tasting and learning about Australian wine. "I meet a lot of winemakers from all over Australia," says Kham, "and I have learned a great deal from them, from how the wine is made to how to cellar and how to serve wine with Thai food."

Kham lives with his wife Tess, son Kristopher and daughter Katherine near the Arun Thai in Potts Point, Sydney. The restaurant has won many awards from the Thai Restaurant Association and won praise in the Sydney Morning Herald newspaper's 2003/04 Good Food Guide for its authentic style of Thai food and its wine cellar.

A brand new feature of the restaurant is the Crying Tiger Bar serving *Khap Klaem*, tapas-style bar food – Thais might love tradition but they also crave change and excitement, too!

Acknowledgements

When photographer Ken Martin and I first travelled to Thailand to begin gathering material for this book I did not actually believe it would ever happen. Thais do not have a tradition of writing things down, depending on taste and handed-down techniques for their cooking skills, so I know that my family will be amazed to see some of our family food history and inheritance in print. My grandfather would simply not have believed it possible! I am very grateful to him and my grandmother, and to my parents for their inspiration and support.

Ken and I have returned to Thailand many times and I love catching up with my relatives, including my Uncles Wanchai and Chana who organized our last trip, dropping everything (in the special Thai way) to help make sure we were looked after. Getting lost with Uncle Wanchai and stopping to "parlez with the locals" was a great experience – he lived in America for many years and has a great sense of humour!

When we first thought of this book nearly ten years ago, we were keen to promote Royal Thai Cuisine as at the time, my restaurant, the Arun Thai, specialized in this form of cooking. We are still very traditional in our methods but we also love change and for the daily specials on the menu, all the kitchen staff will often stop work to discuss the authenticity of a recipe as between us we represent most areas of Thailand. Wat and I come from Isan, Ell lived in the South for many years, Kag comes from the Eastern Central region and my great friend and colleague, another Wat, came from Bangkok, so we have had many lively debates. As I said, Thais love change and we have now also opened a separate bar called Crying Tiger, designed by Peter Metro who we would also like to thank for the initial designs for the book proposal.

Sadly, just as we finally had the go-ahead for this book, Wat was diagnosed with cancer and to our very great distress, died within six weeks. This book is dedicated to his memory and to his family in Thailand. He was a great friend and colleague in the business and he was very much looking forward to the opening of Crying Tiger.

In another unexpected turn of events during this book's production, Ken and Alison (Plummer) faced a frightening bushfire all over their mountainous property on the edge of the Hunter Valley, the famous wine growing area north of Sydney. With the fire contained but threatening to sweep back up the hill, Alison was trying to focus on writing the introduction for the book but found herself understandably distracted. Trevor Winn, the wise Fire Captain (and an artist) from Laguna Volunteer Bushfire Brigade took one look and diagnosed writer's block and, when he and partner Seb had to make a dash down to the creek to rake-hoe a protection line, Alison wanted to join them. "You stay here and write and I want three paragraphs finished by the time I come back," ordered Trevor – putting the writing back on track. Our joint thanks to him and Seb and to all at the Wollombi Bushfire Brigade. Also to Michael, Carol and Ella, and to Lee and Bruce for their input and support.

On the food side I would like to acknowledge the great suppliers of the fresh produce we prize so much in Sydney including fish from the fantastic Sydney Fish Markets and the vegetables sourced by Nida suppliers from Australian growers who produce everything from the large quantities of chillies we use to the fresh herbs such as lemongrass and Thai sweet basil. Also to the suppliers in Thailand who make Thai cooking possible around the world including the dynamic C&A Products coconut milk factory, the Rungroj Fish Sauce Development Co. (represented internationally by W.K.M. International) and the many others exporting Thai ingredients and helping to make our food better known internationally.

A big thank you to Thai Tourism and to Thai Airways for their support and to all those who helped myself, Ken and Alison on our various travels in Thailand. Also thanks to Wetaka Nitikitpaibool at the Thailand Consulate-General in Sydney.

Very special thanks to the editors at New Holland in London, particularly Rosemary Wilkinson and Clare Hubbard, who gave us the opportunity to be published in the first place and patiently worked with us to make the book happen.

Thank you to my staff and the customers at Arun Thai and Crying Tiger and, of course, my special thanks to Ken Martin and Alison Plummer and love to my family who put up with me and my busy life at the restaurant – my wife Tess, son Khristopher and daughter Katherine.

www.arunthai.com.au